How To Read the Bible Aloud

Oral Interpretation of Scripture

by
Jack C. Rang

*A completely new and fully revised edition of the
renowned classic by*
Charlotte I. Lee
Oral Reading of the Scriptures

PAULIST PRESS
New York and Mahwah, N.J.

ACKNOWLEDGMENTS

The Publisher gratefully acknowledges use of the following material: excerpts from The Jerusalem Bible, copyright © 1966 by Darton, Longman & Todd, Ltd. and Doubleday, a division of Bantam Doubleday Dell Publishing Group, Inc. Reprinted by permission. Excerpts from The New English Bible, copyright © the Delegates of the Oxford University Press and the Syndics of the Cambridge University Press, 1961, 1970. Reprinted by permission. Scripture quotations are from the New Revised Standard Version of the Bible, copyright 1989 by the Division of Christian Education of the National Council of the Churches of Christ in the USA. Used by permission. All rights reserved.

Book design by Nighthawk Design

Library of Congress Cataloging-in-Publication Data

Rang, Jack, 1940-
    How to read the Bible aloud: oral interpretation of Scripture / by Jack Rang.
        p.   cm.
    Includes bibliographical references.
    ISBN 0-8091-3493-4   (pbk.)
    1. Bible—Reading.   2. Oral interpretation.   I. Title.
BS617.R36 1994   94-19054
220—dc20   CIP

Published by Paulist Press
997 Macarthur Boulevard
Mahwah, New Jersey 07430

Printed and bound in the United States of America

Contents

Contents

Preface

TO BEGIN WITH . . .

> No one should ever be bored hearing scripture read aloud!
> Our primary task is to see that the words of the Bible
> become living realities for our congregations.

Faced with such a statement, you may be even more unsure of your role as liturgist or lector than you were before opening this book. You may have been thinking about the responsibility of reading "the Word" before an audience ever since you agreed, perhaps in a moment of weakness, bravado or pressure from your pastor, to serve as worship leader for your congregation. And you may not be sure of where to start.

This book was written for you!

It came about as a direct result of the influence of many people to whom we are deeply indebted. The first of these people, paradoxically, are those who read the Bible as if it were a series of dead (and deadly) quotations. It is they, clergy and laity alike, who make one yearn to hear the Bible read fully, intelligently, energetically, even passionately.

We have all heard lectors—both laity and clergy—who do read the life back into biblical texts. And we are often surprised at finding new vistas of meaning as life is breathed back into texts that have become almost shopworn in their familiarity. In the hands of these readers, such used and abused passages became vital and dynamic again.

How do these people do it? Are they just "born with the knack" of reading aloud well? Did they have some super-quality speech class in school that gave them this ability?

Perhaps training has something to do with it, but there is more than reading technique involved. An old school of reading method, called "elocution," made tricks of rate and intensity of speech the standard for performance many years ago. But today's listeners, accustomed to polished (and some unpolished) performances on television, have more sophisticated tastes. They listen for content and understanding from the reader, not just a manipulated (and manipulative) performance.

Now, it is true that some people do seem to have a natural gift for effective oral reading. And some, though certainly not all, speech classes can help individuals develop their abilities in this craft. But regardless of gifts or training, you can learn both to understand and to re-animate the narratives, poetry and drama that comprise the library we call the Bible.

We believe that the Bible, like all other great literature, must be read aloud to realize its full potential.[1] And when our minds are engaged in the content of the text, our voices will provide the informational/verbal communication. Then our bodies are free to provide equally important non-verbal signals to our listeners. It is this combination of verbal and non-verbal messages, along with clearly understood biblical/textual meaning, that makes a lection dynamic. What follows here was written to help you meet the challenge of reading the scriptures aloud and reading effectively.

If you serve as a lector, a liturgist, or a worship leader, we believe you will find some new insights into the mechanics of oral reading. You will find techniques which will help you enhance the devotional meaning and the emotional impact of the worship services in which you participate.

The information on these pages can also provide new approaches for seminary students in need of assistance in preparing for their task of proclaiming the good news—godspel.

We believe it will also prove to be of value to members of the ordained clergy who have found that their seminary training has not provided them with sufficient understanding of the techniques of oral reading. What is suggested here are ways which will help to integrate dynamic reading of the Bible into sermons, homilies and personal ministry.

So this book is for anybody who is somewhat acquainted with the Bible—a person who finds that acquaintance pleasurable. If you have found the sharing of biblical reading with others a satisfying and challenging experience, we believe you will find ways to enhance your skills in these pages.

There has been no attempt here to engage in exhaustive technical explanation of oral performance technique for its own sake. The theory of oral reading has been kept to a minimum. Some attention is given to the reader's use of both voice and body, since voice and body make up the twofold instrument through which we communicate with each other. There are other texts available for readers who wish to do further study in these fields. Reference is made to several such texts in the course of the book.

Some of the chapters deal with the literary qualities characteristic of the various types of writing in the Bible. Our purpose here is to encourage deeper comprehension and fuller appreciation of the literature when it is read aloud, whether for our own pleasure or that of our listeners. The approach is directed to a re-creation of the text—to the demands of the page before us, not to what someone has written or what has always been said about that page. From our experience as teachers, trainers, and from our own work as liturgists/lectors/worship leaders, we believe that any person with intelligence and the desire to do so can read scripture aloud and read it convincingly.

The samples chosen for analysis and discussion have been drawn from numerous versions, including the King James, The Torah, the Revised American, The Anchor Bible, The New English Bible, The Jerusalem Bible, and the Revised Standard Version. We are grateful to the publishers of these versions for their permission to quote from them. We also owe large debts of gratitude to both pastors and laity for their thoughtful reading and comments which opened our eyes to some new vistas of biblical scholarship and to intelligent reading style.

From the clergy, our debt must begin with Fr. Lawrence Boadt, C.S.P., our editor at Paulist Press. Without him, his belief and encouragement, the book would never have been done. And most special thanks to Karen Schialabba, the lady who was far more than an editorial assistant on this venture. Karen was always there when we needed an answer or a lift.

Fr. James E. Heft, S.M., Ph.D., Provost of the University of Dayton, was both a dear friend and a constant source of encouragement and support. To him, many thanks.

We extend deep thanks also to Rev. Dr. Miley E. Palmer of the

Central Illinois Conference of the United Methodist Church, Fr. Paul Soukup, Ph.D., Associate Professor of Communication at Santa Clara University, Rev. Norman E. DeWire, President, Methodist Theological School of Ohio, Janet Larsen-Palmer, Ph.D., President, Centers for Communication Excellence, San Dimas, CA, and Rev. Emerson Colaw, Bishop, United Methodist Church (ret.). These special people read and reviewed the book, shaping it in significant ways. Charles Bartow, Ph.D., Princeton Theological School, pointed out some important "adjustments" which made the book more accurate. Rev. Lawrence Hard, Rev. Dr. Tom Boomershine, and Rev. Dennis Benson all brought unique insights which shed light on the subject at hand.

Then there is our debt to members of the laity. There are special people to whom we are indebted. Florence I. Wolff, Ph.D. and Larry Lain, Ph.D. come first to mind. We owe a debt to Ms. Janine Warisse, whose help with some of the illustrations was invaluable. Other colleagues at the University of Dayton brought yet another angle of vision to the lection process.

The list would not be complete without special thanks to our "in-house" editors, Mary Ruth Rang and the late Ellie Hough. They added fresh fuel when our flames burned low.

The Gospel of John begins: "In the beginning was the Word." The Word is the beginning and end—the reason for our work as leaders of worship.

Now the Word is in your hands and on your lips.

Let it fill your life and light your world.

Note

1. Robert Alden suggests that the Bible has been analyzed so much in recent years that it is time readers simply opened the pages of the Bible and opened their minds to the treasures that pour out from the books. See *The Bible as Literature*.

1

The Scriptures and Oral Interpretation

Throughout this book you are going to meet a word you are sure you know but it will be used in a way you may never have thought of. The word is "interpretation," which has a lot of different meanings, as you would find if you looked it up in a dictionary. In these pages we will be using the word in its academic sense, as it is used in the field of speech. There it is usually referred to as oral interpretation and broadly described as the "reading aloud of a literary text." While there are many different uses for it, in the pages that follow we will define the term by saying that *oral interpretation is the art of sharing with an audience a work of literary art in its intellectual, emotional, and aesthetic entirety.*[1] That last phrase, suggesting that we must know a passage in its "intellectual, emotional, and aesthetic *entirety*" may be a bit frightening. Can we *ever* know any work in its entirety? The answer, of course, is, "No, we can't, especially if the literature is good." In the case of study for the oral reading of the scriptures, the phrase might better read that we will "share with an audience as much of the intellectual, emotional and aesthetic entirety as is available to us *at the moment of reading/performance.*" The Bible produces new insights with every reading, but, as readers, we can only share our insights as far as they have taken us.

How do we do this? If we were being formal we would say: "The act of sharing is accomplished by a voice and body operating under a disciplined and informed mind that is cognizant of the structural elements and the thought patterns in the piece of literary art." We might add that we must share the way that all of these elements operate together to produce a total achievement. But this is just a rather ornate way of saying we know how the ideas and the sentences work together to change thoughts, habits and lives. Armed with that knowledge, we share as much of the work as we can with an audience.

From these definitions it should be clear that we see oral interpretation as much more than just a series of performance "gymnastics." An effective liturgist is concerned with literary analysis—awareness of form and understanding of content—as well as with the techniques of personal vocal and physical projection. She or he is also, to some extent, controlled by emotional or empathic responses from the listeners.

Throughout this book we will be using the terms interpreter, reader, lector, worship leader, liturgist interchangeably, remembering that the reader does more than simply translate written symbols into sounds. In the reading we become the medium through which the written symbols reach the minds—and the emotions—of our listeners, whether they be a few friends or a large formal audience.

At the outset we need to be aware that when we read the Bible we have at our disposal a library of the world's greatest literature. This library includes works of poetry such as the Psalms, drama, and narrative prose in both scriptures. You will find narratives telling of the heritage, history, law, and even the love stories of a special people. There are the dramas of Jonah and Job as well as the dynamic dramatic events which formed the life of Jesus and his disciples. But we have an advantage that other oral readers of literature do not have. For the most part, our audience is predisposed in favor of the book. Given these two factors, quality of material and audience acceptance, it is obvious that we have a responsibility to both the book and to the audience.

Our work as worship-leader/interpreters is re-creative. It is similar to the task of a musician playing the work of a composer. We, too, take the symbols which have been put down on the printed page, and by thorough analysis, painstaking rehearsal, and strict discipline in the use of both our bodies and our voices, we try to bring to life the images that flowed from the creative mind of the writer. We also bring our personal experiences, insights and our study of the text to bear on the clues which the writer has given. And those personal experiences and responses supplement and blend into the literary order imposed by the artist.

We are sometimes faced by translation problems. We may find ourselves involved in the theology of a passage or its exegetical setting.

But our primary interest will be in sharing a selected text with our listeners. In the process of that sharing we will become concerned with what classicists call "rhetoric." For the Greeks of the fifth century, "rhetoric" was defined as the use of language for persuasive purposes. Since what we are sharing is persuasive and instructional in content, we, too, are involved with the term. Like the rhetoricians we are interested in proper handling of voice and body. We are also concerned with the literary style of our lections. And we are very interested in the selection and arrangement of the ideas the passages contain. A major difference between our task and that of the speech-makers is that we do not create, but *re*-create. The tasks of literary style and arrangement of ideas have already been done for us by the author. It is our job to discover all the elements the author has used. Then we must bring techniques of voice and body to the service of those ideas. Only in this way can we share the totality of the selection with our audiences and try to produce appropriate responses.

The Interpreter as Communicator

All phases of communication must have four basic factors: a communicator, a message, a receiver or receivers, and the effect of the message as the receiver understands it. The effect will take the form of some physical, mental or emotional response. Obviously these four factors operate in interpretation as well as in public address, homiletics, theater—in fact, in all phases of speech. But the interpreter must go beyond the usually accepted meaning of the term *message*. It is at this very point that too many people go astray when reading religious and biblical material. The "message" is there, certainly, but it is not always simple, direct persuasion intended to produce overt or even logical response. Our task is not merely to bring a message to an audience but to bring an *experience* which can be shared. More often it is our responsibility to set a mood or bring about an indirect response from the audience. And that sort of response is often centered more on listeners' emotions than on their intellect. To produce that response, we as interpreters must be concerned with every phase of the communication process.

We begin with written symbols, since we are using literature which

3

has been put down in print. We translate those printed symbols into speech sounds as we present the literature orally.

We communicate not only with the words, but also by visible, non-verbal, language, i.e., gestures, facial expressions, empathy, perceived muscle tone, and all the elements of bodily action which are visible to the audience. And, in another aspect of "non-verbal" communication, we shape the speech sounds through the use of inflection, rate, pitch, timbre and other aspects of the physical, speech-producing chain. Theorists tell us that at least sixty-five percent of an audience's under-standing and evaluation of speech messages is based on the *non-verbal*—the visual and the vocal aspects of the communication process. From your own experience you are quite well aware of how these non-verbal elements—a speaker's body and manner of speaking—influence the audience's understanding and acceptance or rejection of the expe-rience being shared.

We have little influence over the first of these stages, the communi-cation by written symbol. The author or authors have arranged and selected language to fit the persuasive end they desired. But the second area—communication through the use of various aspects of *nonverbal* language—is totally our responsibility. The situation is complicated by the fact that there are really *two* communicators involved: first the author and then us, the liturgists. The two speakers must be in as per-fect accord as possible, saying the same thing in the same way, in order for the audience to receive the message and act on it.[2]

Getting at the Meaning

It would be absurd to spend time and space listing arguments to prove that the Bible is successful literature. It has been accepted as such for centuries. Our task is to do justice to that literature. Scholars agree that much of the Bible was originally created orally rather than in written form. Consequently, we must deal with three influences at work in the written symbols which appear in our Bibles. First, there is the mode employed by the speaker—the method and the meaning of the section we are reading. How and why did he tell this story? Second, how well did the reporter/author understand the events of the story? Is the speaker in the work credible? Do we trust his integrity when he reports an incident which he did not personally witness or take part in? The final part of the triad has to do with the comprehension, integrity, and scholarship of the *translator* whose version we have selected.

How was the story told? We know that some of the material was sung, as in the Psalms. In the Christian scriptures we are given reports of the words of Jesus as those words were set down by people who heard him or who had the words reported to them at a later date. In the Hebrew scriptures we are often dealing with a narrator, who probably was not present, but who is reporting Moses' and the prophets' words to the people as those words came down by word of mouth to him. In order to deal effectively with any of the above, we must have some knowledge of the religious, political and economic history, geography and social customs of the time. Our knowledge of these other areas will enrich our reading for a congregation.

Translations

In presenting portions of the Bible orally there are two complicating factors in our attempts to fully understand the written symbols. The first of these is the matter of translation. As they were set down in their original form, the oral and written symbols do not mean much to most of us. So we are fortunate, and grateful, that biblical scholars have translated/transferred those early written symbols into forms that are understandable to us today. This does not absolve us from further study. Whatever we can learn of the original meaning of the words will sharpen our appreciation of some of the troubling passages and the allusions and metaphors as well. Consulting concordances and commentaries will be invaluable here, since knowledge of this sort helps us understand and appreciate some of the literary puns and the acrostic psalms. As is true with any foreign language, puns really do "lose something in the translation," but our awareness of those plays on words does help us to understand the careful workmanship on the part of the original authors.[3] Our primary problem with translation usually has to do with the selection of that one which most completely suits the occasion. When used as part of a worship service, the wishes of the pastor or person delivering the homily or sermon must also be considered. Is there a translation that person wants to use as a base for the message of the morning? The audience must certainly be considered. What are their expectations and theological persuasions?

5

But our immediate concern as we read must be with the *literary* rather than the theological analysis of the selection. We must be concerned with the universality of the *experience*. And we need some knowledge of both biblical and liturgical history. With these in hand we can move on into literary analysis, focusing our attention on the demands of the words we find on the printed page.

Biblical References

The second complication, mentioned above, concerns us directly. As lector/readers we must deal both with unfamiliar allusions and archaic references and, paradoxically, with familiar references. Often we do not need to explain obscure references specifically to our audience unless understanding of the total selection depends on that knowledge. But we as readers must know, for instance, the importance of geographical references—cities of great power or arid desert lands—and of allusions to people and ceremonies that had historical or ritualistic connotations for the time. These awarenesses will enable us to give the proper emphasis and associational value to our reading. Conversely, a *lack* of such knowledge may well produce an intellectual "hole" in the fabric of the text. Audiences have an uncanny way of sensing when we don't know what the reference is.

Lections and Fragments

Another obstacle to a vital and compelling reading of the Bible is the practical need to break the books into lection-sized readings for worship services. This practice often leads lectors to neglect the total context from which the section is drawn. Such disregard can obscure the obvious intention of the passage. This practice can present problems both in the Hebrew and Christian scriptures. When a fragment or a section is used as a lection unit, it is important that we keep it within the framework of the chapter or book from which it is drawn.

The need to clarify the purpose of the writing is probably at the core of the customary divisions of the books of the Hebrew Testament—law, history, prophecy, and so forth. These categories can only provide us with general guidelines. There are numerous overlappings and too many different types of writing to be of much consistent help within these very large classifications. Whether we are reading from the Hebrew or Christian scriptures, we will rarely be using more than a segment of a book. We must plan our reading based on what we find in that particular segment, but we still must see it in terms of the book as a whole. The writer of the passage has already dealt with the problems of word choice and organization. It is important for us find out how each detail works in the total selection. Then we must decide what we must do vocally and through our attitude toward the passage to make the selection achieve its total effect. Only after we have done some literary analysis can we turn our attention to vocal and physical techniques.

Then there is the problem that our audience is at least somewhat familiar with a lot of the material we share with them. They have certain preconceived notions about how these passages should sound. And precisely because the audience does already know "what it's about," we must use all of our knowledge and our skill in performance to make those familiar passages new, vital and alive. The fact that certain faults of delivery are so often ingrained in the audience—monotony of pitch and pace, and the "biblical tone," does not mean that these faults must be perpetuated.

If the selection is worth reading at all, it is worth the effort to see that it catches and holds the listeners' attention. It is in the area of recapturing the vitality of the Bible that there seems to be the greatest need for a fresh approach—to viewing the Bible as *literature*. Biblical research has concentrated so much on what is being said that the importance of how it is said has been all but forgotten. Many readers of scripture become so fascinated by footnotes and commentaries that they lose sight of the *form* and *content* of the literature.

The Bible is made up of a wide variety of literary forms. In later chapters we will look at the characteristics of some of these forms and the way they manifest themselves in certain familiar sections of the Bible, since each one makes its own demands on us as readers, and there are innumerable differences and variations among the selections. It should be clear, then, that we cannot approach any reading of religious literature with a narrow, stylized pattern of vocal delivery and physical technique. Nor can we approach these readings with a mind that is content with categories such as narrative or poetry. Each selection must be analyzed for what it contains in terms of its own

7

organization and its own style. We must look at all of the elements—
the variety, the contrast, the climaxes, the sound values, and the dramatic elements that make up each selection.

Let's be clear about one thing right now—

There is no ONE correct way to read religious literature.

Perhaps no other area of literature has greater need for both flexibility
and control in making use of various types of literary criticism. We are
obliged to bring a lot of "outside" considerations to bear as we work
toward our understanding of the selection. But whatever scholarship we
bring to the passage selected, it is finally *the text which appears on the
printed page* which must be our guide. After we have made our choice of
translations, we are committed to what we find before us. We must
remain faithful to what is on the printed page. Our concern is with what
has been put down and how it has been ordered and formed.

The Art of Oral Reading

Art has been defined as the systematic application of knowledge and
skill in effecting a desired result. In reading biblical literature the
result we seek is the effective communication of the Word of God.
And that communication occurs as a result of preparation so thorough, so painstaking, and a technique so well-coordinated with the
demands of the material that the listeners cease to be concerned with
the reader and focus their attention solely on the material—on the literature itself.

Implicit in the whole process is a sincere and honest desire to share
the experience of the passage with an audience. Without this impulse
to share there can be no vital communication.

The process of sharing begins with the writer, the creative artist. He
orders ideas, words, sounds, allusions, and all the other elements of
style into appropriate form. In the case of biblical literature, the identity of the writer or writers has often been lost or has been questioned
over the centuries. Nevertheless, someone took on the creative task,
and our concern here is with the message and the order in which the
message is presented rather than with the individual himself.

Earlier in our discussion of the four factors in communication we

8

said that the effect of the message on the receiver may result in physical or psychological action or both. This fourth factor is essential to the completion of the process of communication. But in order for the circle to be completed the communicator must have a desired effect in mind. Literature may be written to clarify, to instruct, to inspire, to exhort, to persuade, to praise, to comfort, to entertain, or to achieve a combination of two or more of these purposes. So the questions we need to ask now are: Is the purpose of the communication simply to provide information on which the listener/receiver may act? Is the purpose to change the opinion of the receiver? Is this a "clarion call to action"? Should the listener be moved to do something as a result of the message? In the presentation of biblical material the purpose may be any one of those objectives listed above. To determine that goal, we must take our cue from the author. We must begin with a careful, thoughtful reading of the passage to be presented. What clues are present? Did the selection move us one way or the other when we read/heard it the first time? Examining the literature and then bringing our own thinking into line with the perceived effect is a first step.

Reference to commentaries and concordances may help to take the process further. What have the scholars said about the purpose or significance of this reading? Method of organization, choice of words and referential material, and the use of the tone and sound values of language are all clues to the author's intention and attitude as shown in a selected translation. A reading of the synoptic gospels shows us that the authors not only selected different events and details from Jesus' life, but also selected very different words to describe those events. Each gospel reflects the individual writer's preoccupation with different aspects of Jesus' personality, his life, his teaching, his resurrection, his humanity, his divinity. Further, the writing also reflects the particular position each writer held in relation to the early church itself and the problems it faced at different times and places. Then, too, the gospel writers were writing for different audiences; Matthew wrote for Jewish Christians while Luke wrote for Greeks.

Logical and Emotive Content

The intellectual or *logical* content of a piece of literature is primarily "what it means." It is here, on the *meaning* of the selection, that we as interpreters of biblical and religious literature bring all our knowledge of theology and history to bear. We do this in order to explicate and clarify the material for our listeners. Beyond the basic denotation or dictionary meaning of the words as they relate to each other, there are more complex matters of allusions and connotations. And these are made more difficult because of changing modes and mores in language.[4]

The emotive content evolves from that quality in the writing which produces responses of pleasure or pain. It comes from those words which stimulate an audience to reflection, hope, contentment, fear, joy, gratitude, or any emotion or combination of emotions. In its simplest concept emotive content might be said to embrace the "how" of what is being said. And in re-creating literature, the "how" grows directly out of the "what."

It must be remembered that logical content and emotive content are interdependent. Words seldom have meaning independent of connotative associations. They seldom hold emotion-arousing qualities independent of intellectual association. Consequently, except for the process of analysis, the emotional content and the intellectual content cannot be separated. The degree of their relative importance in any given selection will vary greatly, depending in part on the purpose of the original writing and the purpose for which it is being used with a modern audience. Consider biblical uses in rituals such as marriages, funerals, prayer and Bible services. Both traditional and personal preferences enter into choices there. Nevertheless, it is our responsibility to use everything we find in the selection while exercising care that we are not violating or negating the totality which the author has given us.

Having found as much in the reading as we can at this time, we then allow ourselves to experience it emotionally, relying on clues found in the writing. We bring our experience and our knowledge of human nature with us, then we apply the test of relevance. Our personal, subjective response is legitimate only insofar as it is completely and clearly relevant to the clues we have been given by the text. Then work with voice and body may begin. Then we begin to share the total relevant response with our audience in an attempt to elicit the same responses from them.

As soon as all the written symbols and their relationships are clearly understood, we are ready to move to the second phase: communication by nonverbal language—use of the voice and body. Often during this phase we will experience a broadening and deepening of our first comprehension of the written symbols.

Although some may hesitate to agree completely with Marshall McLuhan that "the medium is the message,"[5] the way in which an idea is expressed is certainly part of its effectiveness. McLuhan's interest, of course, extends from the printed page into other forms of media. Nevertheless, the principle involved is a valuable one and is applicable to literature, as well as to us as we become part of the "medium." It cannot be said too frequently that we are responsible for everything to be found on the printed page whether it is psychedelic typography, poetic structure, or archaic references. And both voice and body must transmit the total work appropriately.

BUT . . .

You cannot communicate what you do not know.

The literature of the Bible is not just something to be reported. The way in which ideas are expressed is often the Bible's most important attribute. It is not enough to know what a selection is about. It is not enough to know what it means. We must also know *how* it means what it means. We must be aware of every technique at the writer's disposal so we can accurately evaluate and use his principles of selectivity. Total knowledge of what and how and why are the only safe guides for our own techniques.

Notes

1. See Charlotte I. Lee, *Oral Interpretation*, 7th Ed. (Boston: Houghton, Mifflin Co., 1987), p.3.
2. Wallace Bacon uses the term "coalescence" when discussing this idea. He describes "coalescence" as coming ". . . from the Latin word coalescens, meaning 'growing up together,' 'growing together as the halves of a broken bone grow together.'. . . When we look at performance elements such as rate, pitch, diction, tone, volume, we need to remember that they, too, must coalesce, and that the performer and work ultimately must coalesce."

11

Wallace A. Bacon, *The Art of Interpretation*, 3rd Ed., Holt, Rinehart and Winston, 1979, p. 43. (Italics added.)

3. It is not the intention of this study to enter into the many controversies about the authorship of the various books of the Bible, fascinating as the subject is. We shall accept the printed page of whatever version we are discussing as the basis from which to work toward a literary analysis.

4. As interpreters our task is often to try to discover what a word or phrase meant to people who can no longer tell us directly. Societies often assign unique meanings to seemingly simple words. The word "red" is but one example, having connotations of blood, fire, danger, anger, politics and others which you can easily bring to mind. Our current lexicon contains a great many words for which the dictionary does not provide adequate contemporary explanations.

5. *Understanding Media: The Extensions of Man* (New York: McGraw- Hill, 1964).

2

The Use of Body
and Voice

In the last chapter we talked briefly about the relationship of the message, the medium, and the receiver or receivers. For us the message we deliver has its origins on the printed page. This is the heart of our communication.

On the simplest level, the medium is the arrangement of letter symbols on a page. When we process those symbols, they translate into words with meanings and connotations. And the transference of those meanings and connotations to an audience in a public setting is our task at that moment when we become the medium. Through our perceptions and our experience we try to translate the written symbols into sound and sight symbols as we attempt to convey the meaning of the text to our listeners. Our means to accomplish this is through our voices and our bodies.

Because voice and body are the basic parts of the interpreter-as-medium concept, this chapter will concern itself with a few simple suggestions for improving both of these aspects of your communication. Some of the material may be familiar to you. If so, we suggest that you use it as a checklist for measuring the degree of control you exercise in your present performance techniques, making whatever adjustments you find necessary. If not, perhaps the techniques suggested will be of value.

One of the problems we mentioned in chapter 1 is that both you and your audience are quite familiar with many passages of the Bible. By practicing some basic performance techniques, then checking to be sure you are being both honest and accurate with the material, you can regain the freshness of those passages. Even if you are reading the

Bible aloud to yourself (and, incidentally, this is the best way to read both for understanding and for vocal clarity) or if you are reading to one or two friends, some of the suggestions that follow will increase both your pleasure and your effectiveness as a reader. If you are sharing the passages with a group, such attention is vital.

In the paragraph above we used the word *techniques* several times. For many years this word carried with it the idea of artificiality—something external to the work. The feeling was that the audience was being impressed by the work of the performer rather than seeing the work *through* the performer. In performances, both past and present, this concept of "going to see the star show off her/his tricks and stylistic devices" was—and for some people still is—primary. In such cases the text itself became a very secondary reason for audiences to attend the performance. Modern interpreters have come to realize that some degree of technique is necessary. Discipline of both voice and body is essential if we are to help our congregations come to a realization of the content of a biblical passage. "Technique" in this case becomes a method, a means of procedure in the creation of an artistic work. It also is a measure of the expertise with which the text reaches an audience.

The *Oxford Universal Dictionary* lists as one definition, "Manner of artistic execution or performance in relation to formal or practical details. . .; mechanical skill in artistic work."[1] Clearly, the more skillful the technique the less obvious it is; and the more it contributes to the totality of the art object, in this case, the Bible passage being read. But the word "mechanical" in the dictionary definition offers some potential problems if our communication is to be effective. Any display of physical or vocal virtuosity for its own sake distracts from the material it should be supporting. While obvious "technique" is in poor taste for modern audiences at any time, it can be a real barrier to understanding in the reading of lections from the Bible.

It is the text, the literature itself, which is important. A conscientious liturgist uses technique to communicate the literature; the literature is not used as a vehicle to display the talents of the reader. Like an exhibition of calisthenics or a recital comprised only of musical scales, we might be interested for a minute or two, but the technique invariably interferes with our purpose—which is to share a significant part of the Bible as fully as we can.

For us, attention to physical and vocal technique should be confined to times when we are rehearsing. During performance our attention must be concentrated on the material at hand and on trying to get, as nearly as possible, what the author wanted in response from the listeners. If we have prepared adequately, our muscles and our voices will respond according to the habits we have developed during practice. As skill and experience increase, those habitual responses will become more natural. Then we will need only an occasional practice/evaluation session to be sure we have not picked up any mannerisms which might distract our audience, making them concentrate on us rather than on the material.

As worship leaders we need to work on communication techniques in the same way that a musician practices scales. Just as a musician cannot give a satisfactory performance without having first perfected the handling of his instrument, so we as lectors, who are both the instrument and the instrumentalist, cannot do justice to a selection unless we have devoted some attention to the tuning of our physical/vocal instrument.

Using Our Bodies in Performance

Studies done over many years have shown the interdependence of an individual's voice and body. Our voices simply will not function at maximum flexibility and effectiveness without understanding and practice in control of the physical mechanism. With this idea in mind, we begin with some suggestions on physical control for maximum effectiveness in oral performance.

Most beginning liturgists assume that we only communicate with others through the use of our voices. The truth is that what we see is often far more vivid, more response-producing, than what we hear. Nonverbal communication—the visible language of the body, as well as the intonations and inflections of voice—often underscores or contradicts verbal, spoken language. "Body language" often reveals our attitudes toward ourselves, toward those we are addressing, toward the material we are trying to communicate.

When our attention is self-directed and on the impression we are making we radiate clues that alienate audiences. It quickly becomes clear to them that we are not interested in the selection or the sharing of the selection but only in demonstrating our own histrionic abilities. An audience is quick to resent a "holier-than-thou" facial expression or the "wiser-than-thou" posture or the "more-inspired-than-thou" gestures. They are also quick to question our authority if we seem unsure of the material. Sometimes such impressions are the result of habits we have formed by imitation of someone we have seen or heard in our early churchgoing years. Often these habits are so firmly established that we are no longer aware of them. Some religious speakers seem to have been trained in "if not holier, at least better-than-thou" attitudes in seminary. As a result, their ability to communicate is usually hindered rather than enhanced, because these attitudes distract congregations from the purpose of the reading. They put up barriers to the very responses which the writer of the book or passage was trying to produce in his audience in the first place.

Our communication with our audience begins very early. From the moment an audience is aware of our physical presence at the lectern or pulpit, they begin to make judgements, establishing mental and emotional acceptance or rejection of us and, incidentally, of our scriptural message. And the majority of these judgements are made on the basis of those *physical* actions and attitudes we express. It includes the way we sit; we are being judged before we even stand up.

Bodily action, defined as "any muscular movement," may be as large as a full gesture or as small as the tensing or relaxing of the muscles around the eyes, the mouth, or across the shoulders. It may be any combination of these movements. It includes a whole range of movements from that moment when we approach the platform and it continues until the moment we are seated again. It includes movements of our head, arms, shoulders, hands, and legs. Shifts in foot positions and balance, changes in posture, facial expressions and the whole muscle tone of our bodies all make up "bodily action."

In earlier days the elocutionist/reader had to learn a whole vocabulary of gestures and stances which were thought to convey emotions to an audience.[2] Today we certainly do NOT need that elaborate array of rules for posture and gesture. We know that the test of effective bodily action is how it works in the sharing of the material at hand. Nevertheless, we are constantly working to strengthen and control our physical actions.

Too many readers attempt to communicate from the neck up.

Genuine sharing involves the entire body working as a unit to serve the material. How much bodily action is enough and how much is too much? Physical response works when the action is so unobtrusive that it goes unnoticed except as it contributes to total response to the text. It works when the audience is not distracted by personal or habitual mannerisms.

Posture

The basis for effective bodily action—and for good voice production—is good posture. And good posture is primarily a matter of a proper relation between the parts of the body. Good posture can be defined as

> that arrangement of bones and muscles which results in perfect natural alignment, each unit doing its appropriate job of supporting and controlling the body's structure.

Barring any physical defects, good posture or alignment requires nothing more complicated than standing relaxed and straight from the ankle bone to the crown of the head so that the skeletal structure falls naturally into balance. This is not as effortless as it sounds, however, if bad posture habits have been allowed to develop.

Because the muscles of the body are easily trained and adjust themselves rather quickly even to misalignment, errors in balance, slouching or rounding the shoulders may be firmly established without any apparent tensions or strains. One of the most common posture problems results from allowing the spine to sway in at the center of the back. This permits the neck and head to be thrust forward and the pelvis to be tilted out of natural position as we try to maintain our balance. Not surprisingly, this sort of posture seriously affects effective speech. The throat muscles tighten as a result of the thrust position of the neck. This interferes with vocal flexibility. Muscles across the base of the ribs are tightened, inhibiting good breath control. Sometimes compensation for such posture is effected by thrusting the chest forward. This encourages shallow breathing and places added strain on the delicate throat muscles. At the opposite extreme the spine is allowed to curve out so that the shoulders droop forward, the chest sags and the pelvis tips forward, causing the stomach to protrude.

This results in crowding the important diaphragm muscles and cutting down on breath capacity.

The secret of standing straight is not the old familiar "hold your shoulders back" admonition of our adolescence. The shoulders should be held easily and naturally on top of the rest of the body. If the spine is straight, the shoulders will tend to assume their proper position and the chest will lift slightly, causing the large muscles of the abdominal wall to be drawn in. Your head should be held in easy balance, neither protruding forward nor tilting back out of alignment.

Obviously, during your reading, you do not hold your head rigid, nor any other part of your body for that matter. But an occasional check on the crown of your head, shoulders and spine alignment will give you a balanced, flexible, responsive and coordinated body.

> A very simple and comfortable way to check on your body align-
> ment is to lie flat on the floor (NOT the bed; it is too soft and will
> conform to your present posture errors) and stretch as far as you
> can, pull from your toes to the crown of your head. Relax your
> shoulders and arms. Become aware of the part your feet must play
> in the coordination of your whole frame. Then, when you stand,
> force your muscles to remember the "all in one piece" feeling which
> you developed during the few minutes on the floor.[3]

Often in an eagerness to reach the listeners, a speaker will develop the habit of leaning forward from the waist. Or will emphasize a point by thrusting out both the chin and shoulders. These postures sometimes make listeners feel they are being pushed at, and they will immediate-ly retreat. The opposite extreme of bending back from the waist sug-gests that the speaker is trying to escape, keeping as far as possible from the audience. The response is obvious: Immediate tune-out. A too casual slouch not only suggests indifference but also cuts off full control of breathing.

These are all postures which have become habits with some speak-ers. They may be effective for certain occasions and certain passages, but they must not become so set as to become habitual and invariable.

Muscle Tone

"Muscle tone" refers to the degree of tension or relaxation present in your body. A properly poised body is flexible, responsive, coordinated and fluid. As we said above, it is "all in one piece." When your posture is good, your body is in a state of controlled relaxation with no undue muscular strain or tension. Note that we said "*controlled* relaxation." Controlled relaxation is not to be confused with lack of physical energy. Quite the contrary. If we look too tired, depressed, or bored to stand up straight we communicate a negative impression to an audience. Relaxation is an easing of tension; it is not total disintegration.

We used the word "poised" a moment ago. The word is usually defined as being in a state of equilibrium, a state of balance. So a poised body is relaxed, controlled in accordance with the demands of the material with which we are involved. In the same way, balance between the parts of a lection itself determines our degree of bodily tension or relaxation. Muscle tone is affected by our mental attitude as well. It will vary from obvious tension to assured, controlled relaxation, all in direct proportion to our confidence in our material, our audience and our preparation for both. Every performance carries with it a degree of excitement which is translated into physical tension. The secret is to channel that tension so that it becomes an asset rather than a liability. The "butterflies" in the stomach which indicate tension are not a sign of fear but of excitement. And when properly controlled and understood, that excitement communicates itself to the audience in terms of a vital, stimulating performance. Too often, however, an inexperienced reader attributes this tension to stage fright—and immediately sets up a fear pattern which blocks successful communication. If the material is good, acceptable to the audience, and the preparation has been adequate, then the "butterflies" will fly in formation as an indication of a level of excitement and not fear. They are the result of our involvement in the literature, without which our reading cannot succeed. Of course, if we have not spent enough time in preparation and are really unsure of our ability, or if we are not sure that we have done the best we can, then there is neither hope nor sympathy for us. We cannot hope to solve the problem until we are willing to put sufficient time and effort into careful and complete preparation. How much time is enough? When you have "done your homework" on the background of the material and have become familiar with *every word*. When the whole reading flows smoothly in rehearsal.

A word of advice about rehearsals: Short twenty-minute rehearsal sessions yield more return than one or two long ones. You give the reading a chance to grow in your mind and your heart between rehearsals.

Gesture

Gesture 1. a movement or movements collectively of the body, or of part of the body, to express or emphasize ideas, emotions, etc. [4]

For us as lectors gestures are overt actions limited to the hands and arms—and occasionally the head and shoulders. And these parts of the body function as a result of our study and our physical and emotional response to a particular emotion or action taking place in the reading. They are an intellectual/emotional "follow-through" which affects and is affected by muscle tensions throughout the body. For this reason it is impossible to talk about gesture apart from our awareness of posture and muscle tone in general. Unlike those readers of the last century who were trained in the theories of "elocution," we are not concerned with gesture as a separate and separable part of our training. Rather, we believe that gesture is an integral part of bodily action and that it grows out of our responses to the material. Gesture is a complement—an aid to—complete communication. If an action does not help communicate the material, it has no place in the reading. It becomes a distracting, extraneous movement which violates the basic principle that nothing we do should call attention to itself. This is not to say that gestures are not to be used. We are saying that their use must be dictated by the needs of the material being presented.

Whether or not we use gestures usually depends upon two considerations. The first, as we have said, is the material. We will use whatever bodily action is necessary to clarify the meaning and to effectively convey the emotional quality of the selection. We are attempting to create a *total impression* in the minds of our listeners. So we use bodily action to supplement language and help our audience re-create what the author has put down. Too many or too specifically planned gestures are likely to call attention to us and distract the audience from the text-material we are attempting to vitalize.

The second consideration in the use of gesture is our own personality. Some readers respond more physically or more easily than do others. If gestures are difficult for you and make you self-conscious, forget about them. Concentrate instead on your empathic responses and muscle tone as you read. You should use whatever gestures you wish in practice until you can handle them effectively when you need them, but you should never let gestures become an issue when you are before an audience. There is nothing more distracting than an empty gesture appliqued to a reading—a feeling that the word "GESTURE" has been written on the margin of the script—and that you are responding to something you do not truly feel. When your concentration shifts from your material to the problems of gestures, your audience will sense your preoccupation and tune out.

On the other hand, if you are one who talks with your whole body, by all means use those gestures which come naturally, the ones that make you feel at ease, the ones that help you communicate with your audience. There is the danger that gestures which are comfortable for you may distract your audience, so you may need to try out your reading with a trusted friend as your audience. Ask that person if your gestures were a distraction or if they blocked communication.

In some cases readers have developed certain habitual physical actions which are not gestures at all in the sense of helping to express a feeling or an idea. A person may be repeating a movement, such as constantly raising and lowering one hand or tilting her head or shrugging his shoulders for no apparent reason, at least for no reason that seems significant or motivated by the reading. Unfortunately, many of us have grown up watching just such cliché-actions, since religious leaders are some of the worst offenders in the use of these "stock" movements. Under ordinary circumstances, it is not advisable to practice a reading in front of a mirror because in doing so you are likely to separate physical response from its proper function in communication. If, however, you suspect that you have a too-regular pattern of movement, an occasional checkup before a large mirror will help call your attention to the fault.

As we have said, a really good reader does not plan specific gestures. A passage is never marked to cue the use of a carefully worked out movement at a particular place. Rather, we strive for such complete understanding of the material that muscle responses and gestures will be automatic, complete, and will become an integral part of the reading, without our planning and often without our awareness of them.

A good gesture conforms to no rule except the rule of effectiveness. It is effective when it helps to communicate a feeling or an action, when it is unobtrusive, and when it does not result in distracting mannerisms. A good gesture depends upon and grows out of our total response to the material. Like every other aspect of technique, gesturing must be the result of our mental and emotional response to what is on the printed page. As such, it will be a powerful force in creating corresponding responses in the listeners.

Empathy

One of our subtlest and most powerful tools is to be found in the control and use of empathy. Although its roots are in classic Greek, *empathy* is a term borrowed from modern psychology. It is literally a "feeling into," a projecting of oneself into the mental, emotional, and physical state of a person or persons in a work of art. This mental projection of ourselves into a piece of literature implies, of course, *emotional* response to the writing as well as logical comprehension of it. Do not confuse the term "empathy" with "sympathy." Though the literal meaning of "sympathy" is feeling *with* someone or something, the term is more usually defined as feeling *for* someone—"I feel so sorry for that poor, homeless child." Empathy, on the other hand, says, "As I read this, I physically hurt with cold and hunger along with that child." Dylan Thomas says, in one of his poems, " And I saw in the turning so clearly a child's forgotten mornings . . . That his tears burned my cheek/And his heart moved in mine."[5] This is ultimate empathy.

Every writer who deals with emotions to one degree or another uses words and phrases that may cause us to react. The words may produce pleasure or pain, activity or repose. As liturgists, it is our job to respond to these cues, these phrases and words with both our minds and our muscles as we prepare the material. If we have not precisely experienced what the author is describing or creating, we can usually recall some situation which was either parallel or at least similar to it, a situation which evoked a comparable response. Emotional response and physical response are closely related; one intensifies the other. Though we may not have been consciously aware of it before, our muscles do, in fact, tighten or relax as we mentally and emotionally respond to written or orally presented material. If, for example, I tell you that I am going to scrape my fingernails across a chalkboard, and the sound upsets or irritates you, simply the *suggestion* of the action will make your neck muscles tighten and your toes curl—even though you did not hear the actual sound. Of course, the change in muscle tone affects the tone of the whole body.

A word of warning: The muscular responses you make are the result of inner, mental activity; they are never a substitute for it. The mental or emotional responses must come first; the muscular response will follow. There are two types of physical/muscular response material in every work. They are often classified as a part of that area called imagery. The first type is called *kinetic*. It pertains to large, sweeping overt action. The second, the one most relevant to our discussion here, is called *kinesthetic*. It pertains to interior muscular tension and relaxation. This last type is usually directly related to empathy. The use of kinesthesis is one of the oldest storytelling methods known when an emotional story is being told.[6] For example, there is a strong empathic response—including a kinesthetic tightening of muscles—to the primarily visual imagery of "And when Aaron and all the children of Israel saw Moses, behold, the skin of his face shone; and they were afraid to come nigh him" (Exod. 34:30 King James). There is a lot of other imagery, kinesthetic and otherwise, in Eliphaz's speech to Job:

> Now I have had a secret revelation,
> > a whisper has come to my ears.
> At the hour when dreams master the mind,
> > and slumber lies heavy on man,
> > a shiver of horror ran through me,
> > and my bones quaked with fear.
> A breath slid over my face,
> > the hairs of my body bristled,
> Someone stood there—I could not see his face,
> > but the form remained before me.
> > Silence—and then I heard a Voice . . .
> > (Job 4:12-16, The Jerusalem Bible).

Look at all the images! The *sound* of a whisper, the heavy *feeling* that comes with sleep, the *feeling* as a shiver runs through us, the feeling as a "breath slid over my face." There all sorts of imagery shifts from one sense to another. And the passage is held together by the responses we, as readers, make to the situation. We must suggest those responses using both our voice and our body. Imagine the effect the memory of this experience had on Eliphaz as he recalled it. Consider also why he related the incident to Job. It should be clear that the passage cannot be read as if Elphiaz was saying, "Take my advice, Job."

Probably neither we nor our listeners have ever had an experience even close to the one Eliphaz describes, but all of us have had some experience of the sensations described in these four verses. Our listeners will probably not be consciously aware of the physical ways we reexperience and re-create the images, but they *will* respond to our muscle tone, voice quality, and pace. (Check the endnote above about performer/audience interaction.) The experience becomes more intense for them as they share the experience with us, Eliphaz, and with one another.

The Bible is full of complex imagery such as this, and we will consider the uses of imagery again later in this chapter. So the first step in developing empathy with a selection is to determine our full mental, emotional, and physical response to a piece of literature. Without this total response, the second step is impossible, because . . .

The second step in empathy concerns the audience's response to the reader's presentation of the material. As we observed, this response usually takes the form of an unconscious imitation of the speaker's muscle tone. When we, as lectors, are responding empathically to our material, we give physical cues to our listeners, who in turn respond by muscular imitation. It is this muscular imitation that helps intensify their emotional response. It is the same phenomenon which causes us to frown and feel depressed or irritated, to smile and feel happy, to yawn and feel tired or bored because someone else is frowning or smiling or yawning. Being aware of this imitative aspect of empathic response is of vital importance to us as lectors. As listeners, we are often robbed of the simple comfort or joy of some of the words of the Bible because what we see and hear from the pulpit—and imitate within ourselves—is an attitude of pomposity or condemnation or disinterest instead of understanding or dignity or joy.

To be effective, we, as good worship leaders, learn that there is empathy inherent even in the way we approach the platform or lectern. A sense of urgency or reluctance, quick or slow movement on our part can provide the congregation with an empathic association between the reading, themselves, and us. During the introduction we try to use empathy to help establish an emotional state of readiness within the minds—and the muscles—of the audience. They, by unconscious imitation of what they see from us, will adopt the physical tone that makes them ready to receive the emotional responses which are being communicated. Psychologists have varying theories to explain empathy's sources and effects. We as lectors, however, are primarily concerned with how it works in the interaction of the reading, first with us when we prepare, then when we present it, and then within the members of our audience when they receive it.

Finally, we need to be aware that the current of empathy runs in both directions. We receive a stimulus from the audience just as they have received it from us and from the reading. In communication theory the term for this circular flow is "feedback." The pattern begins with the mind of the author as he expresses it on the printed page. His ideas flow to us. We transmit the emotion/idea to a group of listeners. They, in turn, react—sometimes audibly—sending their emotional energy to us, adding a congregational response to the reading. The important thing for us to remember is that effective reading of scripture is a community event; an event we share with our parishioners.

Sense Imagery

Much of our physical and emotional response to literature comes from imagery which appeals to our senses. "Imagery" has been variously defined. Perhaps the least valuable definition came from a university professor who referred to imagery as "The reconstitution of prior experience, minus only the original initiating stimulus." We can find a more practical definition in Shakespeare's Henry V when the Chorus, speaking to his audience, says,

On your imaginary forces work.
 Suppose within the girdle of these walls

25

Are now confined two mighty monarchies
Whose high upreared and abutting fronts
The perilous narrow ocean parts asunder;

. . . .

Piece out our imperfections with your thoughts;
Think when we talk of horses, that you see them
Printing their proud hooves in the receiving earth . . .
For 'tis your thoughts that now must dress our kings,
Carry them here and there, jumping o'er times,
Turning the accomplishments of many years
Into an hour-glass."[7]

So, "imagery" is an author's way of reminding us of things we have seen, heard, felt, tasted, touched.[8] As we noted, the author reminds us of how a situation feels both physically and emotionally, through the words he has chosen to represent that scene or action.

Imagery is divided into categories: *visual*, appealing to sight, *auditory*, appealing to hearing, *tactile*, to touch, *thermal*, to heat and cold, *gustatory*, to taste, *olfactory*, to smell. It is important to remember that the senses seldom work independently of each other. A word or phrase which appeals primarily to sight, for instance, will probably appeal to another sense as well. For the moment, however, it is well for us to remember that all of our impressions of the world and most of our basic knowledge of it has come to us through our senses. Writers use imagery which appeals to those senses to sharpen our perception and make relationships more vivid. They most frequently use sense imagery in their descriptions of persons or places or things. We need to be aware of those images and respond to them fully in order for our *listeners* to respond. Look again at the many sensory images in the passage from Job cited earlier.

Eye Contact

This is a good time to talk about eye contact. If you have had a speech course, or if you have observed good speakers, you have undoubtedly heard the maxim that to be effective in public address you must look your audience in the eye. Now you are faced with an audience for whom you will be reading gospel lessons and stories. "How," you ask, "can I 'look 'em in the eye,' read intelligently, and be an effective worship leader/reader? I can't look at the audience and at the text at the same time without memorizing the material—and I have a terrible memory!"

We know from personal experience, and from the experience of other lectors, liturgists and worship leaders that it is both possible and preferable that you maintain a *degree* of contact with your congregation *at all times* when you are presenting scripture in a worship setting. And part of that contact is, in fact, direct eye-to-eye relationship with your listeners. Part of the relationship is achieved through your knowledge of the text. Part is achieved when you become the personae, the characters in a biblical story or the prophet-reporter-narrator from the past.

While we will explore these roles in more detail later, it is good at this point to pass on some tips about how you can become familiar enough with your reading(s) to get your eyes off the page at least part of the time you are presenting the lection material for the morning.

Type out a copy of the material you are going to read.

Why not use the Bible you always bring with you? Two reasons. First, typing/copying the material makes you more familiar with it. You become aware of every word and the order of every word in your lections. You discover words the meaning of which you are unsure—words you need to look up in a dictionary, a commentary, or to consult with your pastor. You get the flow of the language—whether the sentences are short and terse or long and involved, with lots of dependent clauses.

Second, the type is larger and, since we recommend you double space the copy, it is much easier to read than the fine and rather closely-spaced print in most Bibles.

Perhaps even more importantly, the typescript becomes your "working copy" as you prepare. You can underline important words; you can put all sorts of markings on it to guide you. You will rehearse with it. And this is the copy you should take to the lectern with you on Sunday morning.

Another use for this typescript, and a technique used by many truly good readers of scripture, is to carry the script with you throughout the week, looking at it whenever you can. While this "occasional reference" idea does not replace regular rehearsal, it does familiarize you more and more with the texts as the week goes by. One friend says that, using this technique, he is able to proclaim the gospel without reference to his copy during the service.[9] Now, you may not be able to reach that level of skill in the first couple of tries, but the more you do refer and practice, the more you will find yourself free of the page, able to look or not look at your audience as the scripture dictates.

Why not "look 'em in the eye" all the time, if I can? As Wallace Bacon points out, some literature is very public—very much to be shared with the audience. A narrator who speaks directly from the page, like the narrator who, in Matthew's gospel, tells us about the events leading to Jesus' birth, shares his insights eye-to-eye with each listener. At other times these same speakers look at and describe a scene or visible elements in the story which they want us to see through their eyes.

The important point here is that PRACTICE is the key to effective reading. And a lot of *short* rehearsals are more valuable than one long one. Why? Because a lection, like every other kind of good literature, is *alive*. The experience of the reading will continue to grow in your mind and your performance every time you come back to the reading. So, the way to effective worship leadership is "practice, Practice, PRACTICE!"

Notes

1. *Oxford Universal Dictionary*, prepared by William Little, revised and edited by C. T. Onions, 3rd Ed. (1955: Oxford at the Clarendon Press, Amen House, London), p. 2140.

2. Unfortunately, the practice still persists in some lectionary and gospel reading advice pamphlets and books. Notes inserted in passages indicating that the words should be read with "slowly building intensity" or "higher energy" are simply attempts to produce prefabricated, "cookie-cutter" readings, with no room for individual understanding and personal involvement in the texts.

3. A dancers' exercise, which they also call "alignment" is worth your attention. Check some of the texts on movement for theater and dance for the "Rag doll/suspended string" techniques recommended there. The results are the same—a straight spine and comfortably positioned arms, head, chest, back and legs.

4. *Webster's New World Dictionary of the American Language, 2nd College Edition* (Springfield, Mass.: G. & C. Merriam Co., 1971), p. 587.

5. "Poem in October," from *The Collected Poems of Dylan Thomas*. Copyright 1953 by Dylan Thomas, copyright 1957 by New Directions.

6. According to S. Singaravelu (cited by Judith G. Martin, S.S.J), seventh/ eighth century Tamil dancers in India "helped in bringing about what is now known as 'kinaesthetic process' i.e., the mental or emotional state of the singer was 'translated' deliberately into dancer's movements which when perceived by the onlooker aroused in him sensations of muscular sympathy, and these in turn associated themselves through memory with mental or emotional states which would have produced similar muscular effects in his own experience. Thus ideas were conveyed from the mind of the bard to that of his audience not only through the words of his songs but also through kinaesthesis brought about by the dancers of the bardic troupe."

"Tirumular and the Tamilizing of Saivism," in *In Spirit and in Truth: Essays Dedicated to Fr. Ignatius Hirudayam*, S.J., Madras, India: Aikiya Alayam, 1985, pp. 141–2.

7. Wm. Shakespeare, *Henry V*, Act I sc.i. Emphasis added.

8. A more detailed explanation of imagery is to be found in the *Princeton Encyclopedia of Poetics and Poetry*, edited by Alex Preminger, and published by Princeton University Press. See pages 363 to 370 in the 1978 expanded edition.

9. Members of his congregation regularly comment on the vitality and sense of newness even familiar passages take on when this man "proclaims the Word" in all its fullness.

3

The Roles of Voice and Diction

In the last chapter we focused on the development of flexible body response when dealing with sensory imagery in a lection. We suggested, also, some of the effects of physical, bodily response on vocal technique because they do work together. Body and voice are a twofold instrument, and we must learn to control them both so that they combine to convey whatever the literature demands. As we have seen, the body makes its own special nonverbal contribution to our message. But it is our voices which are basic to our communication as worship leaders. Unless we can be heard and understood, muscle response and appropriate gesture offer very little toward a sharing of the text.

For informal communication and conversation our everyday voice serves adequately. But the oral reading of scripture requires additional flexibility and more specialized control. The fact that you use your voice every day, and have done so since you were a child, is no guarantee that it is an adequate instrument for the more complete communication required by some of the difficult and demanding passages found in the Bible.

Breath Control

The first concern of anyone interested in voice improvement should be breath control. Without it the production of any vocal tone is impossible. And effective use of the normal breathing mechanism is really simple. Any difficulties are usually due to bad habits we have acquired over the years. Now, there are times when physical or psychological tensions inhibit normal breathing, but occurrences of this type are relatively rare. When we understand the muscles involved in the breathing process—and the functions they perform—we can often locate and release any tensions we find in our own breathing-for-speech.

On inhalation—the intake of air—the major concern is with the amount of air drawn into the lungs. In exhalation—the release of the air—the concern is with control of the flow of air. The whole process of breathing depends on the physiological and physical principles of the balance of tension and relaxation in opposing sets of muscles that serve to control the creation of a vacuum.

When the diaphragm (the large dome-shaped muscle which forms the floor of the chest cavity) *contracts*, it lowers and pushes downward against the relaxed abdominal muscles, increasing the lengthwise expansion of the chest. This drawing may help you visualize the action:

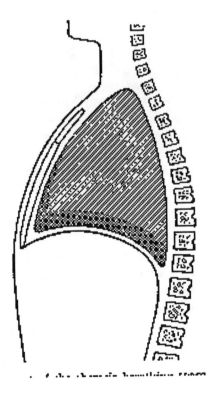

As you can see, while this action is taking place, the muscles between the outer surfaces of the ribs contract. The rib cage then lifts and extends, producing a side-to-side and front-to-back expansion of the chest. This increase in size creates a partial vacuum inside the chest cavity (the more darkly shaded area in the drawing above). To fill this vacuum, the pressure of the outside atmosphere forces air into the space, equalizing the pressure inside and outside the body. The air is forced down the windpipe (trachea), on through the bronchial tubes, and finally into the flexible air sacs in the lungs, where the bronchioli terminate. The air sacs in the lungs expand as air enters.

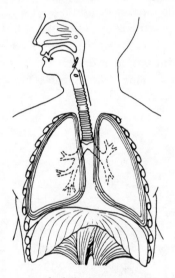

When the lungs are extended the process of inhalation is complete.

We need to be clear about the function of the lungs in the speech-production mechanism. Their primary purpose is to serve biological functions in the body; their use in speech is almost always secondary to our personal well-being.

Once filled with air laden with oxygen, the lungs exchange that oxygen, replacing it with carbon dioxide which the body has accumulated in the metabolic process. When the mechanism is ready for the process of exhalation—releasing the transferred carbon dioxide—the muscle fibers in the diaphragm relax, and the diaphragm rises, returning to its original dome-shaped position in the chest. The muscles on the outside of the rib cage relax as the ones between the ribs on the inside contract. This action pulls the extended rib cage inward. All this pressure upward and inward acts upon the elastic lung tissue containing the air. The elastic tissue begins to collapse, and the air is forced out of the lungs, up through the bronchial tubes, through the windpipe, and finally out of the nose or mouth. One cycle of respiration is completed. And, on the average, your body goes through this same process twenty times a minute.

In exhaling for *speech*, however, there is frequently another action in addition to the relaxing of the diaphragm in the lower chest area. This other action is the firm contraction of the abdominal muscles which were relaxed for inhalation. As they contract for exhalation, these muscles support the action accomplished when the diaphragm is relaxed, and in this way help to control the flow of air. It is simply an additional action, or rather a continuation of an action, in the process of exhalation during silent breathing. From this description it should be clear that breathing is a very active muscular process.

If shortness of breath has bothered you during previous oral performances, you obviously want to develop greater breath capacity and better control of exhalation during speech. The first thing to remember is that proper breathing begins with proper posture. If each muscle is to perform its assigned function, your body must be in a state of equilibrium—of controlled relaxation. That is, the muscles are in a balance between relaxation and essential tension. Note the word "essential." Wrongly induced tension restricts the flexibility of muscles that control the intake and outward flow of air. Holding your body in a state of tension and rigidity cuts down on breath control enormously. One symptom of such tension comes from forcing the muscles of the rib cage and abdomen into a "locked" and rigid position. They must be firm, but they cannot function if they are locked.

Improving Breath Supply

In exercises for improving breathing habits, it is particularly important to have your spinal column erect but not forced into position. Your shoulders should be level, and the muscles that support them should be free from tension. Trying to increase breath volume by lifting your shoulders during inhalation only serves to put tension in the wrong area. The price of such tension is that vocal tone is damaged by the unnecessary tension. A simple exercise may be helpful. It will show you how to achieve the proper balance between tension and relaxation in the special muscles of respiration. This exercise will also show you where the concentration of your energy should be—at your "beltline" rather than in your throat.

1. Contract your abdominal muscles *sharply* and force the air out of your chest on a single vocalization such as "Ah- -h- -h," much as if you were sighing. Hold the contraction of these muscles a moment, then *suddenly* release the tension. Notice that air rushes into the chest and fills the lower part (perhaps more) of your lungs on the release of the tension. Now exhale by forcing air out of the chest by gradually contracting the abdominal muscles as the diaphragm is relaxing and returning to its dome-shaped position.

2. Repeat the process you just completed (Step 1), and as the air rushes in on the release of tension in the abdominal muscles, make a conscious effort to lift your upper rib cage slightly (careful that you *don't lift your shoulders!*). This slight lifting will help to create more space in your upper chest, and the whole chest will be well extended and can now accommodate more air. The upper portion of your lungs should now be filled, as well as the lower portion. Now exhale, pushing the air out by relaxing the diaphragm and gradually contracting the abdominal muscles and lowering your rib cage. Don't collapse and let your shoulders sag!

3. Now, repeat the process described in step 2. After you push out all the air, take another full, deep, easy breath. A you start to exhale the full breath, begin to vocalize by counting aloud. As you start to run out of breath for vocalizing, gradually contract the abdominal muscles (*not* the upper chest ones) as you continue counting. You are now using "forced exhalation." When you can no longer force air out of the chest by the strong but comfortable contraction of the abdominal muscles, *stop* the vocalized counting. Don't sacrifice good quality of tone in an effort to squeeze out more sound. "Squeezing" like this results in undue tension in the upper chest and throat muscles—and that is exactly what you most want to avoid.

This basic exercise for developing good breath control should be the starting point for any period of exercise. You should not work steadily at this or any other exercise if you begin to feel tired. Until you grow accustomed to the new method of control, or find that you have achieved a marked increase in capacity, go back to your usual manner of breathing for a "rest." It should be increasingly clear, however, that the more often you do this type of exercise, the sooner you can make this method automatic. Then you will discover that the whole breathing-for-speech process will have become easier.

As you are able to take in larger amounts of air with ease and continue to fully support a tone, you should be able to count more numbers on one breath. Try to increase the count with each exercise period. But always take care not to strain your throat, forcing the tone, or sacrificing good quality. Count at what seems an easy volume for you, and at a comfortable level of pitch.

No experienced speaker will ever start to address an audience without taking a moment to get a full, easy, satisfying breath. Of course, this must be done subtly so that it does not call attention to itself. You can do this in the few seconds you spend waiting for the audience to settle and focus their attention. You can also check on your posture. Taking a full deep breath will also calm your nerves amazingly well. It works for major league baseball pitchers; it will work for you, too. Then, when you inhale properly, you will be surprised at how much more relaxed and confident you feel.

Now you can breathe wherever the material demands a pause; you will not have to pause in order to breathe. It is usually impossible to get a full capacity breath except in the major pauses that complete the units of thought. Therefore, the final step in control of breathing is to learn to inhale quickly and quietly while still using the proper muscles.

Controlling the Flow of Breath

Frequently a speaker inhales properly and uses full breath capacity, but still is unable to sustain a long flow of sound. Here the problem is not one of insufficient supply of air but of improper control of exhalation. This is one of the major causes of dropping volume on final words or syllables preventing them from carrying to the last row of the audience. Another simple exercise will help you determine whether

35

the control muscles collapse or if they exert steady pressure as they relax:

1. Inhale a full, comfortable breath. Hold a lighted match (a wooden "kitchen" match works best) directly in front of your lips as close as your profile will allow. Start to count aloud in a full voice. You should be able to continue until the match burns down. If you blow out the flame, check the control of the muscles in and around the rib cage. Most of us exhale more than we need to on certain sounds, such as "*two*" or "*th*ree" or "*f*our."

2. Light another match, take another deep breath, and repeat the exercise, speaking very softly with conscious control of the rate of relaxation of the muscles involved. You will feel as though you may explode, but you won't, and you will be made aware of where the control must be exercised. As you gradually increase your volume to normal, you will find that the match will flicker but, by controlling the flow of breath you will not extinguish it with a sudden burst of air.

These two inseparable factors in communication are so important that they are always of major concern to oral readers, actors, or professional speakers.

Volume and Projection

You undoubtedly have been in an audience of average size, and found to your distress that you could not hear the speaker, so you already know the immense importance of sufficient volume and good projection. After all, the interpreter's primary purpose is to communicate the material to the audience. If you cannot be heard, you have failed in your primary objective.

Actually, the terms *volume* and *projection* are sometimes used interchangeably, and they are both part of a reader's ability to be heard and understood. For greater clarity , however, let us consider volume as *degree* of *loudness* and projection as *the act of directing your voice to a specific target.*

Of course you must be able to make your voice fill the room in which your listeners are gathered. You must learn to control volume in order to fill that space easily without distorting your voice or blasting down the back wall if space is limited. You must know how much volume is required to reach the people seated in the last row of the room and how to achieve the greatest possible flexibility within that space requirement. Your knowledge of the entire breathing process is basic to your control of volume.

Focus of Projection

It is sometimes helpful to think of your voice as a tangible thing—something to be directed and tossed at a target. The trick of "throwing" your voice may sound a bit like ventriloquism, but it is a practice we all use. A child calling to attract the attention of a playmate down the street does it. If you are a football or basketball fan you have "thrown" your voice by shouting instructions or encouragement to the players in the game. And we direct our voices in these situations often without conscious thought to the exact spot where our attention is focused. When you are carrying on a conversation in a room full of people, you may have been aware that you had to project your voice across the room to answer a remark or add your bit to a conversation over there. When you want to be confidential, you let your voice drop, and you narrow the circle to fill only a desired area.

Here are some exercises for focus of projection that you will find effective if you practice them in a large room. They are designed for concrete situations, enabling you to concentrate on the volume and focus suggested.

1. You are seated at a desk in the center of a room. You see a friend at the door; you call an easy greeting. She waves and goes on. You think of something you ought to tell her. You call her name, but she apparently doesn't hear, for she keeps on going. Without leaving your seat, call again; have a good full breath as you start to call and direct the sound at her fast-disappearing back. Do the same thing again, with more volume and longer sounds supported by forced exhalation. Be sure you catch her this time.
2. You are giving directions to a group of people who are working on a problem. The room is large and everyone must hear. Direct

your remarks to various places, thinking of certain people who might be there. After you have given instructions and the group starts to work, a question arises down in the front of the room. You shift your focus, and answer the person who asked the question. You then decide that others might need that special information, too. You raise your volume and expand your area of projection to attract everyone's attention, then repeat what you have just told the individual. As you do this, take care to direct your voice to various parts of the room so that everyone will hear you.

3. Think of your voice as a ball which you can toss to various parts of the room. Aim it carefully at the far corner. Next let it drop onto the floor in front of you. Then send it with a strong thrust to another part of the room. Be aware of how your mind takes the aim which your voice follows. This is a useful principle to recall from time to time when you address a small or large audience. Be sure they actually "receive" your message.

Until you get the feeling that you are supporting projection with the big muscles of the diaphragm and rib area, keep one hand on your midriff while you are doing these exercises. Put the other hand lightly on your throat. When you feel the throat muscles tighten, stop and start over making sure that the big muscles "bounce" the voice out. Wherever you are directing your voice be sure the push does not come from tightening your throat.

In working to develop volume and projection, you are concentrating on one of the basic requirements of all speech: that the audience be reached. And volume depends largely on adequate breath supply and proper support in exhalation. Projection combines these physical aspects along with the psychological aspects of mental directness.

Electronic Assistance

Most large churches or auditoriums are equipped with public address systems. Their use can be a mixed blessing, especially if you are not accustomed to working with a microphone. While it is true that these systems amplify the volume of your voice, it is also true that microphones amplify all of the bad features of your voice as well as the good. Too many people who have not had much experience with microphones really do not trust them. Many speakers feel that they must shout over or past the microphone in order to be heard. Our best advice is to get someone to listen while you practice. Set the volume control on the system at a comfortably high level so you will not have to get too close in order to be heard. At first, it will be hard to control your volume. The tendency of most people is to shift away ("off mike") occasionally, which causes a large swing in volume—sometimes soft, sometimes loud. Second, when you lean in and crowd the microphone in most systems your voice will be distorted, sounding "tinny" or metallic and harsh.

Be aware of the *type* of microphone you are using. Don't be afraid to ask if you don't know about such things. The type of microphone the system uses is important to your presentation.

Some are *directional,*

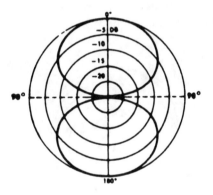

meaning that they pick up sound from only one side or direction. If this is the type you must use, realize that you must stay within the cone-shaped pattern which begins at the front of the mike, the part you are facing. With this type of amplification you will not be able to move around freely or use much in the way of bodily action during the reading.

Some systems use a type of *non-directional* microphone

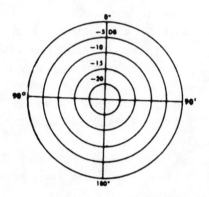

which can pick up sound from the top. Their quality is usually rather poor, so your diction and projection must be better, sharper than ever.

A third, more generally used, type is called a *cardioid* microphone. As the name implies, it has a heart-shaped pattern beginning at the back quarter and circling out to the front.

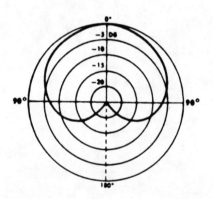

This type is most forgiving when you move and is generally of good to excellent tone quality. Whatever the system, take a little time to learn it and learn to make it work for you. Find the speaking level which allows your voice to carry to the back of the room without distortion. Mere volume, even with the best public address system, is not enough to make your words come through clearly to your audience.

Unfortunately, it is not unusual to encounter a beginning reader/ speaker who can be heard but cannot be understood. Obviously this touches on problems of pronunciation and articulation, which will be discussed in a few moments. But being understood also depends on the speaker's control of projection. True, projection includes sufficient volume to carry the tone whatever distance is required by the material and the speaking situation. But projection also involves the speaker's constant awareness of the listening audience. You must always keep the last row of listeners in mind and be sure your words reach them. It truly does not matter whether your audience is composed of a few people sitting around a campfire or fireplace or hundreds of people gathered in a church sanctuary or auditorium. Your mental attitude toward your communication with every one of your listeners has an indirect but observable effect on your control of projection. Thinking of your listeners, wanting to be sure that they hear and share the full effect of the lection, you will tend to keep your posture erect and your head lifted slightly so that your throat is free from tension.

Pitch and Quality

Although pitch and quality are different attributes of sound, they are so closely related in human speech that we will consider them together. The length and thickness of the vocal bands—or cords, as they are more commonly called—and the way they vibrate basically determines both the pitch and the quality of the vocal tone The pitch is determined by the *rate of vibration* and the quality by its *complexity*. The pitch of a sound, of course, relates to that sound's position on the musical scale. It is generally described as high, medium, or low. Changes in pitch lend variety and richness to the material being read; they also suggest shades of meaning. And all such changes help to hold the audience's attention.

A change in pitch produces *inflection*, and a speaker's inflection range is the entire pitch span between the highest and the lowest tone of which one is capable.

Any pattern in the variation of these pitch levels produces *melody*. When there are no discernable changes of pitch, the result is a monotone. Melody is an asset to the interpreter, but it can also become a problem. Many individuals have a characteristic inflection pattern in their ordinary speech that becomes part of their personality. Impersonators play on these inflection characteristics when they imitate the speech of some well-known person. Inflection pattern is certainly to be expected in every reader, and it will carry over into performance when you read for an audience. In some instances, however, a reader's pattern is so unique that it calls attention to itself and gets in the way of the material being communicated.

Sometimes in our youth we decide our voices are too high or too low, and we set out to change them. In these instances it is easy to develop a false pitch level that strains the throat and will in time cause fatigue and hoarseness. Instead of opening the throat so that the full set of vibrators can operate efficiently, we push the voice down into the chest where it rumbles away on one or two tones, getting in the way of both intelligibility and flexibility. Conversely, in trying to raise or pitch, we mistakenly tighten the throat muscles and speak from the back of the mouth instead of letting the strength of projection and volume come from the larger supportive muscles. And as the years pass we begin to sound childish instead of mature and poised.

A voice must never be pushed from the throat. The small muscles there are not strong enough to support such effort and will tire quickly. If you become hoarse after speaking for a half hour or so, check on the diaphragm support you are giving the exhalation which produces the source of sound. Place your hand across the front of your throat and if you feel the small muscles at the front and sides tense unduly, go back to the breathing exercises suggested earlier. The suggested full deep breath before starting to speak will help relax your throat and put the support where it belongs.

Quality, more difficult to define precisely, can best be described as that characteristic of a tone which distinguishes it from all other tones of the same pitch and intensity. Voice "quality" is sometimes called the timbre, the "ring" of the tone. In describing quality, you may find yourself using words that suggest color—a "golden" tone, a "silver-tongued" orator (to use a term from earlier times), or, in musical terms, a "blue" note. You have already thought of several other words used to describe "quality" in speakers' voices. Quality, then, is the distinctive individual quality of a voice that makes it possible to recognize a friend when you hear him but do not see him.

Quality of tone is perhaps most closely associated with mood or feeling. The connotation, or cluster of associations around the words being read, will help dictate quality. We will discuss connotation more fully in the section on word choice in chapter 4. For the moment it is enough to be aware that the mood and emotional content of a selection are enhanced by an appropriate vocal quality. This quality underscores the connotation of the words the author has chosen to share a particular experience. Quality, like all other aspects of vocal and bodily technique, is a part of a whole, and helps the reader in communicating the totality of the selection to the audience.

Often religious readers unconsciously (it is to be hoped!) adopt what is commonly called a "ministerial tone," or, a "stained-glass voice." It is pompous, it is sleep-inducing, it is deadly dull. It features a pattern that lifts at the end of each minor unit of thought with a rising—drooping—rising double-bending inflection, or circumflex. It has been referred to occasionally as the, "My dear Christian friends," inflection pattern. Another problem pattern is the dull, "this is the Word of God and it doesn't need any attention from me, and besides you have all heard it before" unmelodic pattern. It suggests that you are distancing yourself from your congregation, and anything that produces distancing can be fatal to any sort of vital communication. Concentration on what is being said and how it is put together, coupled with an honest wish to share the total experience of the literature, are the only cures for this occupational hazard. If the habit is long standing the cure will take some time, but it is certainly worth the effort.

The Bible consists of literature about people and their relationships with God and with one another. It has moving and important things to say to us. It presents a wide variety of moods and styles. There is no set, stereotypical way to read the Bible. A reader's vocal and physical techniques must always illuminate the selection being read.

Rate and Pause

The rate or pace at which you speak is often habitual, a part of your personality and your entire background. It probably serves well enough for ordinary conversation, but it may be necessary to adjust that everyday rate to do justice to the style and purpose of a passage from the Bible. As with other elements of vocal technique, you must train your ear to hear yourself in practice and in conversation. There is no magic formula for slowing a too-rapid pace. It requires constant attention. Selecting material with a style and connotation that encourage a slower pace is sometimes helpful. Frequently the mere physical process of forming a sequence of sounds will affect the rate at which a sentence can be read.

Within the overall rate there will be opportunities for subtle and important variety. Emotion, connotation, suggestion, and the combination of vowels and consonants all provide variation in your reading rate.

Rate includes not only the speed with which sounds are uttered in sequence, but also the length and frequency of pauses that separate the sound sequences. A pause may be sustained for a much longer time and with greater effect than you realize, but it must be motivated by clear understanding of the words that surround it. The important element in the use of pauses must always be that the audience can feel that the pause is filled with a thought or series of thoughts going through your mind. It is not just an unfilled spot on the page, a place where you have written "PAUSE." Pauses in a reading are not unlike the blank space between stanzas in a poem[1]; they must indicate that some mental or emotional change is occurring within the material or within the speaker, or both. You need to be sure that something *relevant to the material* is going on during the pause, in your own mind and consequently in the minds of the listeners. A pause should link what comes before and after; it should not be a derailment in the train of thought. When combined with empathy it can be a powerful instrument for the conveyance of emotion, but it must always stay within the total concept of the reading and supply whatever transition or suspense is needed.

In your reading try not only to use pauses where they will be most effective but also to vary and sustain the lengths of the pauses as the material demands. Punctuation, of course, may serve you as a guide to pauses—but it is only a guide. Punctuation is used on the printed page to signal your eye. It guides the silent reader in establishing the relationship of words and phrases and their division into sentences. In your reading you may accomplish the same statement of relationship through the use of changes of pitch or quality or emphasis, or a combination of these, to signal the ear of your listeners. For example, the third chapter of the book of Daniel relates the story of Shadrach, Meshach, and Abednego and their trial in the fiery furnace. The twelfth verse, as it appears in the King James version, gives us the accusation brought against them by the Chaldeans to King Nebuchadnezzar: "There are certain Jews whom thou hast set over the affairs of the province . . . ." When you read this silently the words are quite straightforward. When the late Charles Laughton read this story, however, he wanted to be sure his audience understood that the Jews were not a popular people, especially since they had been placed in positions of power in the country. To emphasize his point, Laughton used a pause—that certainly does not appear in the Bible—and an emphasis, an underscoring, that doesn't appear on the page either. If we were to write it down, the reading would look something like:

"There are certain—JEWS—whom thou hast set . . . ." The addition of a pause and the manipulation of the words "Jews" made it quite clear that, in Laughton's mind at least, these men were already despised and condemned by some of the people they ruled. Pause, emphasis and rate were his only devices. And it worked.

In other cases pause may not convey the message as fully as going on into the next sentence or word. Rules and fashions change in punctuation as in everything else. Your understanding and response to the material, together with your sense of your audience, are the final determinants in the use of pauses.

Intelligibility of Speech

We have already noted that, to fulfill its basic function of communication, speech must be understandable or, at least, intelligible, and that it must be clearly heard. But to be fully intelligible, speech must be more than just audible. It must also be distinct, with clear diction producing accurate images for the audience. Your listeners cannot keep their attention on the content of the material if they are constantly called upon to translate slovenly speech sounds or mispronunciations. There are dozens of dictionaries which provide pronunciation guides of both the English language and the names of people and places in the Bible. With all of these resources available, there is really no excuse, except lack of care in preparation, for failing to pronounce words and names accurately.

It goes without saying that you will always want your words to be distinct and correct as well as pleasing to the ear. It is true that nothing is more irritating to a listener than a speaker's self-conscious, over-careful mouthing of vowels and consonants. It smacks of affectation and insincerity and immediately directs your listeners' attention away from the message of the text and onto you and your performance techniques. On the other hand, if you cannot be understood—if speech sounds are slurred and sounds elided one into another—you certainly cannot communicate. So, you must always strive for habits of pronunciation and articulation that are clear and communicative but unobtrusive. Your speech must be such that any audience can understand you.

Poor articulation, combined with too-rapid rate, produced this prime example of mis-communication:

A student in a speech class was giving a speech about "Goofing Off in College." He finished his first point by saying, "suhrealartchuno." The instructor was puzzled and made a note of the "word." The second point concluded the same way— "suhrealartchuno." By this time the instructor was suspecting some mystical incantation and vowed to listen very carefully as the student sped onward toward a conclusion. When the student repeated the "incantation" the third time, the instructor unravelled it. It wasn't a word, it was a sentence: "It's a real art, you know," "suhrealartchuno!" The student knew what he was saying; it was only the audience that was baffled as he rattled along at top speed, slurring words as he went. Diction aside—a major problem for the audience was that the pauses between the sequences of sound which make up the words were simply not long enough to allow intelligent translation of the message symbols into image/ideas.

We have used the words "pronunciation" and "articulation" frequently in the section above. Perhaps a distinction between the two might be helpful. *Pronunciation* assumes that word-sounds are accurately spoken; it is not immediately concerned with the shaping of the sounds. Dictionaries provide guides to the sounds of a word as well as the proper emphasis of certain sound units. *Articulation,* on the other hand, refers directly to the shaping of the sounds by the speaker's lips, teeth, tongue, and the hard and soft palates. Sometimes it is hard to decide whether a fault is a matter of pronunciation or of articulation. While substituting "axe" for "ask" is a matter of pronunciation in most societies, "He kep' it" for "he kept it," might be either faulty pronunciation or slovenly articulation. On the other hand, when a listener hears a lisping sound—"thithter Thuthy" for "sister Susie"—there is no hesitation in deciding that this is a case of faulty articulation. Pronunciation is considered acceptable when all the sounds of a word are uttered correctly in their proper order and with accent/stress on the proper syllable. Current good usage is the guide to correct pronunciation, with a standard dictionary as the final authority.

Biblical names and places can often be difficult. If you have any doubts, consult a biblical dictionary, an encyclopedia or a concordance. Write out the pronunciation, using your own phonetic style to do so. For example, "Nebuchadnezzar," the king mentioned earlier, might be written out "Neb-uh-ca[d]-NEZZ-er." Practicing with this personal transcription will set the sounds in your mind so that when you see the Bible's version you will remember, and say, your phonetic version. If you still aren't sure, check with your pastor, then write out the pronunciation to be used in the sermon. You both will appreciate having the same sounds for the same word reaching the congregation. Practice the word until you can say it confidently and with full voice. Don't pull back and mutter for fear it will get away from you. If you do, your listeners will be distracted both because they didn't really hear the word and because of your lack of security with it. If you know what correct pronunciation is and you have checked your own speech patterns, you can then turn your attention to improving the formation of the sounds of the words, strengthening their projection.

Faulty projection of distinct speech sounds is closely related to the position of the sound within the word or phrase. The end of the word or phrase is often slighted or perhaps omitted, even though the preceding sounds are clear and distinct. In the exercises for control of sustained exhalation, we pointed out that adequate control is needed to complete and support the ends of lines or sentences. This control and the accurate shaping of end sounds are closely allied. The failure to finish words is one of the major faults interfering with good communication.

The consonant sounds that help most in achieving distinctness are *p, b, t, d, k, g*. They are called the *plosive* consonants because the sudden release of air which completes their formation is a sudden, sharp "explosion" in the air. It is this plosive element that promotes their carrying power. To check your own use of final plosives make up a list of words ending with these sounds, then practice making sure those final sounds are distinct. Words like "respond," "eighth," "good," "gig," "slept," "asked," and "cloud" are some examples; consulting a dictionary will turn up many more. Tongue-twisters using these and many other sounds are too numerous to mention. You undoubtedly are familiar with Peter Piper and his peck of pickled peppers and Theopholis Thistle, the successful thistle sifter. These jingles are excellent devices for practice in accuracy and flexibility.

Watch also the unvoiced plosives, *p*, *t*, when they appear in the middle of words. Check to be sure you say "li*tt*le," not "li*dd*le," "sto*pp*er," not "sto*bb*er," "bo*tt*le," not "bo*dd*le." There are a lot of words that demand careful medial consonant articulation to insure correct communication.

The *fricative* sounds, so called because they escape with a slight "hiss" of friction—*f*, *v*, *s*, *z*,—also demand particular attention to accuracy in their formation. Sometimes, as was suggested in the exercise for control of exhalation, the vigor of the escaping sound needs to be toned down. The sounds that give the most trouble are the ever-present s and z, the unvoiced and voiced sibilants, respectively. Actually, s and z are among the most frequently used, and often confusingly used, consonants in the English language. "S" is a single sibilant sound in "soft" or "silver," but it is a diphthong, "sh," in "sugar," "sure," and a few others. You may need to check your own pronunciation against a dictionary when you encounter lines such as:

> He made the incense altar of acacia wood, a cubit long and a cubit wide—square—and two cubits high; its horns were of one piece with it. He overlaid it with pure gold: its top, its sides. . . . He made two gold rings for it under its molding, on its two walls—on opposite sides—as holders for the poles with which to carry it. . . . He made all the utensils for the altar—the pails, the scrapers, the basins, the flesh hooks and the fire pans: . . . On the north side, a hundred cubits—with their twenty posts an their twenty sockets of copper, the hooks and bands of the posts being silver (Exod 37:25–38:11, The Torah).

If you hear your own "s" sounds too prominently, what is sometimes called a "whistled s," try relaxing your tongue as you direct the sound against your teeth. Or you may need to shorten or cut off the sound by a quicker stoppage of the flow of air. If the sound of s seems too "slushy" or unclear, try to increase your effort to direct the stream of air directly over the center and tip of your tongue. What you are aiming for is to expel the air centrally between the aligned edges of your upper and lower teeth. If you notice, or someone has mentioned, a marked deficiency in the pronunciation of any speech sound you may need to consult a speech therapist.

This discussion of body control and especially of voice improvement may seem unduly detailed. You may never have considered that your speaking voice is a twofold instrument, serving both communication and biological functions. Again, you may already be aware of the things we have touched on. If you believe that your current, everyday speech really is sufficient for the reading of scripture, let us suggest that you wouldn't try to play the organ to offer "a song unto the Lord" if you couldn't manage the keyboard. On the other hand, if breathing and voice control are already familiar subjects, an occasional reminder of the techniques involved is a guard against developing sloppy habits.

Learning to control your voice and body properly for oral reading is not arty or theatrical. It is basic if you are to be successful in direct and honest communication. The person who feels it is presumptuous to use the best possible technique in reading the Word of God has forgotten perhaps to whom he is indebted for that voice and body.

Note

1. See Paul Fussell, *Poetic Form and Poetic Meter*, for a more complete discussion of the use of the spaces between stanzas of a poem.

4

Literary Style

An understanding of the elements of literary style is important to us as oral readers of scripture. By looking at style we are better able to catch the rhythms of the material we are reading. This knowledge also furthers our understanding. Awareness of style takes us well beyond the surface meaning of the words themselves to the ideas the words represent. We gather clues to relationships between events and speakers which, in turn, increase our perception of the nuances of language within a passage. And this understanding enables us to present the selection with greater understanding to our listeners. Awareness of literary style also helps us establish an appropriate pace; it aids in finding proper inflections and pauses, and it assists us in following the method of organization already present in the selection. All of this knowledge helps us to guide our listeners through the reading, because analysis of literary style helps us and our audience see how everything works together to achieve a total effect. And, with these perceptions, we are then able to select those physical and vocal techniques which will do proper service to the lection.

There is one thing a study of style will *not* do. It will not tell us very much about the identity of the often-anonymous author of our reading. For countless years scholars have disputed the authorship of many of the books of the Bible, and a study of literary style will not resolve the question of the author of a given selection with any degree of finality.

What is "style," anyway? Literary critics broadly define style as a reflection of the complex influences of social attitudes and environment that have produced certain patterns of thought in an author, and an habitual vocabulary he uses to express those thoughts in writing. Rather an ornate definition, but the point is that, from a study of style a sense of the personality of the author does emerge, even if his exact identity remains unknown.

Often the style of a selection is generalized. People use words like "reportorial" or "pedantic" to describe the style of a particular selection. At other times such phrases as "rhetorical," "majestic," "flowing," "sweeping," or "staccato" are used. More often than not these words describe the way an oral rendition strikes our ears; they may not truly describe the style of the writing itself. The terms often result from a reader's imposition of his own rhythm and melody pattern on the writing. And often this imposition distorts both the text and its contents. So, in order to discover the "style" of a piece of writing, we must look for clues within the work itself. From those clues we can plan the performance elements, the techniques of vocal communication we have at our command.

We can consider literary style in terms of

1. method of organization by which the total idea is developed;
2. type, length, and syntactical structure of the sentences within the smaller thought units;
3. choice of words and their relationship to one another within particular sentences;
4. division of the sentences into speech phrases as they are read aloud;
5. rhythm established by the speech phrases as a result of stresses and pauses.

We can begin at either end of this list or anywhere in the middle as long as the selection *as a whole* is considered. Each segment affects and is affected by all the others. We cannot separate the various elements of a passage and still produce a total effect that gives the selection its mood, tone, and emotional intensity.

The tradition of fragmenting chapters and books into small sections of a few verses for lectionary purposes has frequently led readers to lose the organization of the book or chapter. This loss, in turn, often brings about a misrepresentation of the attitude present in the whole work, diluting its effect on the audience. For example, there are not too many times when we would be expected (or want) to read one of Paul's letters in its entirety to a congregation, and certainly not at one service. But whenever we read any *portion* of a letter we must remember the tone of the whole letter, beginning with the introduction, and let the influence of that introduction be felt in our reading. If we fail to do so, Paul's affectionate but firm rebuke and his fatherly advice can turn into a near-tirade.

This detailed examination of the elements of literary style is not intended to be evaluatory. It is merely a means by which we come to a more complete understanding of what we will find on the printed page. Our task will be to look carefully at whichever translation we choose to use,[1] then do an analysis which will allow us to see how the elements of style work together to form the whole in that version.

Since the usual designations for the parts of a public speech, i.e., introduction, body, and conclusion, are equally applicable in tracing the pattern of development of thought progression in a piece of literature, and since they give us good clues to this matter of style, we will begin with them.

Introduction

Whether the structure is narrative or dramatic the unifying principle is chronology—things happen in a time-bound sequence of actions. The *introduction* to either form supplies us with essential information about time, place, characters, and sometimes occasion. The Christian scripture parables often compress this information into a single sentence. An example is in the account of Jesus' meeting with the centurion in Matthew 8:5–6:

> When Jesus entered Capernaeum, a centurion approached him with this request: "Sir, my serving boy is at home in bed paralyzed, suffering painfully" (NAB).

In a single sentence we are given a wealth of background information. We are told the place, the reason for the meeting, the relative social positions of the people involved, and some clues to the centurion's character as well as his attitude toward those who were close to him. Armed with these facts, we have all that we need to develop the rest of the story.

Narratives in the Hebrew scriptures are more likely to include significant historical and political data in their beginning passages. They often give us both time and place as well as occasion. A good example is this one, found in Esther 1:1–3:

> It was in the days of Ahasuerus, the Ahasuerus whose empire stretched from India to Ethiopia and comprised one hundred and twenty-seven provinces. In those days, when King Ahasuerus was sitting on his royal throne in the citadel of Susa, in the third year of his reign, he gave a banquet at his court for all his administrators and ministers, chiefs of the army of Persia and Media, nobles and governors of provinces (The Jerusalem Bible).

Here we get the time, set in the reign of this Ahasuerus, (since there was apparently more than one king by that name). We are told the specific point in time where the story begins, "in the third year of his reign." And we learn a bit about the importance of the occasion: The king wants to impress the people in charge of the day-to-day operation of his kingdom. And he wants to show off his prize possession, his queen, Vashti, in all her beauty. We are given no clues to tell us why she refuses to appear. We only learn it is her refusal that leads to her banishment from the royal presence, an action which brings Esther on-stage to become the central figure in the drama.

We certainly must not ignore the political importance of such an occasion as this. To do so is to rob the story of both its human element and its historical significance. And this introductory passage gives us all of the preparation we need to enter into the action of the story which follows. This expository device is a characteristic of all narratives, and all drama as well.

If the writer's purpose is to persuade his audience, the introduction will take whatever form has the widest appeal to that particular audience. Paul's first letter to the church at Corinth contains a masterful use of just such an introduction. He first establishes himself and his position in relation to the Corinthians:

> Paul, called by God's will to be an apostle of Christ Jesus, and Sosthenes our brother, send greetings to the church of God which is in Corinth; to you who have been consecrated in Christ Jesus and called to be a holy people as to all those who, wherever they may be, call on the name of our Lord Jesus Christ, their Lord and ours.

Grace and peace from God our Father and the Lord Jesus Christ (1 Cor. 1:1–3, NAB).

But Paul does not depend merely on stating his own position. He stresses his affection for them, his feeling of kinship with them and his pride in their having been converted, becoming followers of Jesus. He then devotes the entire first chapter to a call for unity and harmony among the members of the Corinthian church. He goes on to point out the differences between divine wisdom (and folly) and worldly wisdom (and folly). Their wisdom, and even their "folly," is, or should be, divine because of their faith. With these words he has set them apart from the less fortunate and less informed people around them. This implication that they are special people is a very effective technique.[2] And the continuing references to his affection for them make the reprimands which follow easier to take.

Frequently when a writer is primarily concerned with clear, incisive thought or with the importance of cause and effect, he uses "lead-in" sentences to introduce each step in the development, linking each unit clearly to what has gone before. Paul is an expert in using this device and can build his case with the logic of a lawyer. Each paragraph picks up an idea, or more often a specific word, from the closing sentence of the preceding paragraph. Then time is devoted to developing that word or idea before finally linking it with the next paragraph.

In this way each chapter, and indeed each paragraph, in 1 Corinthians has its own pattern of organization within the larger structure of the whole. Further analysis of Paul's letters reveals even more examples of how he will elaborate on an idea introduced in a preceding chapter or verse. Each unit has its own introduction, body, and intimately persuasive conclusion leading neatly into the next major unit—which then repeats the pattern. If we pay close attention to the attitude established at the beginning of the letter and to the organizational method which unifies the entire work the *style of the writing* clarifies many seemingly convoluted thoughts, making them more meaningful to us and to our audience.

Within each chapter of the various books of both the Hebrew and Christian scriptures we will find "lead-in" sentences which serve to focus our attention on what follows. In preparing our readings we must take care to use those sentences for the same focusing purpose.

Body

After the introductory unit has accomplished its task, the writer moves into the body of his material, that is, into "the heart of the matter." This is done in several different ways. The writer may take a single thread from the introduction, then amplify and expand on it. A detail or a concept may be developed by presenting examples or taking a closer look at various aspects of the concept. Or the writer may develop that detail into a larger issue. Paul's letter to the church at Rome can serve as an example.

After his salutation and his prayer of thanksgiving for the members of the church in Rome, Paul makes his "thesis statement" which he will follow through to the end of the epistle:

"The one who is righteous will live by faith."

He goes on from there to pursue "The Guilt of Humankind"[3] idea, stating that the wrath of God is against all whose wickedness suppresses truth. Paul outlines the extent of sin in the world, targeting the Jews of the day. He then gives an example to show how "God's Promise [is] Realized by Faith." Next he uses the comparison-example of Jesus and Adam. He draws an analogy from marriage. He continues his argument by saying that "Salvation is for All," and that "Israel's Rejection Is Not Final," that there is "New Life in Christ." He ends his discussion of salvation through Christ in the first four verses of chapter 15, concluding with:

> For whatever was written in former days was written for our instruction, so that by steadfastness and by the encouragement of the scriptures we might have hope (Rom 15:4, NRSV).

In the brief and relatively unfamiliar letter of Jude, which has no chapter divisions, the author wastes no time in getting to his purpose with:

I was already fully intent on writing you, beloved, about the salvation we share. But now I feel obliged to write and encourage you to fight hard for the faith delivered once for all to the saints (Jude 3, NAB).

He mentions the people who are threatening the faithful and, in order that there be no mistake in their duties, he adds "I should like to remind you," then, "Next let me remind you"; and "remember, my friends." The steps in organization are clearly defined as he leads them—and—us from one major thought unit to the next.

In a narrative the body of a book or chapter begins when the plot and action for which the introduction has given us the time, place, and characters begin to develop—when the story gets under way. A rereading of the book of Esther shows this pattern very well. The first chapter and the first fifteen verses of the second introduce the place and the "inciting moment" in the drama when Queen Vashti refuses the king's request to appear at a banquet. The king decides to replace her, and the main theme of the story is underway. From the moment of the king's decision and his words of banishment for Vashti, the plot unwinds to its conclusion.

Conclusion

The third major unit in organization is the *conclusion*, which draws together the principal threads of the introduction and the high points developed in the body of the material, finishing the story. The conclusion may take any one of many forms. It may be a summary, it may be a pattern of deductive or inductive reasoning pointing to a philosophical tenet, it may be a call for action or a significant question growing out of the examination of various factors which have been discussed in the body. These are just a few of the ways a writer may conclude a chapter or book. Since we have been looking at some of Paul's epistles, consider how clearly the conclusions are set off there. He usually concludes by returning to the tone set in the greeting. He begins his first letter to the church at Corinth by saying:

I give thanks to my God always for you because of the grace of God that has been given you in Christ Jesus, for in every way you have been enriched in him, in speech and knowledge of every kind—just as the testimony of Christ has been strengthened among you—so that you are not lacking in any spiritual gift as you wait for the revealing of our Lord Jesus Christ. He will also strengthen you to the end, so that you may be blameless on the day of our Lord Jesus Christ. God is faithful; by him you were called into the fellowship of his Son, Jesus Christ our Lord (1 Cor 1:4–9, NRSV).

And he concludes this letter to the Corinthians with:

Be steadfast and persevering, my beloved brothers, fully engaged in the work of the Lord. You know that your toil is not in vain when it is done in the Lord (1 Cor 15:58, NAB)

From this example you can see how important retaining the tone of the introduction in your reading becomes. Paul consistently returns to that opening tone, leaving it as one factor in his concluding statements. Often there is a formal summation in the form of a doxology as well as a final greeting and blessing. But the bulk of the argument is a development of the thesis set forth in the introduction.

While this is the pattern in the epistles, in other biblical narratives, the conclusion is usually brief. It simply tells us of the action that followed as a result of the climax. For example, at the conclusion of Jesus' temptation in the wilderness, Luke says:

And Jesus returned in the power of the Spirit into Galilee, and report concerning him went out through all the surrounding country. And he taught in their synagogues, being glorified by all (Lk 4:14–15, RSV).

Here time is not a factor; the only concern is with actions. At other times the conclusion simply tells us that the characters left the scene and went to another place.

The book of Esther is unique in that it has, in effect, two conclusions. The first completes the story of the Jews' peril, their revenge, and Esther's part in the ultimate outcome. The conclusion of the book itself establishes the dates of the Feast of Purim and in some versions authenticates the story itself. So the overall organization is one of an introduction, a body, and a conclusion. You will find this sort of organization within the chapters, and in smaller narrative units within the chapters, as well as in some of the books themselves.

It is important to remember that those ideas clustered together in a paragraph in a prose selection or a stanza of poetry usually work in very close relationship to each other. They often form a medley of associated minor thought units. The division into chapters in the Bible is based on this unity of incident. It is helpful in analyzing the entire thought pattern of any biblical story to pay attention to key ideas that tend to be clustered together. You will then be more aware of the contribution each idea makes to the total progression of the chapter or book.

Sentences

The second element of literary style concerns the structure of the sentences within the work. Sentences may be defined as complete units of thought within a paragraph or within a chapter of the Bible. As we read, and become aware of their function for us in performance, the relative length of the sentences in a selection provides some significant insights into the overall style of the work. And later, when we come to read the selection aloud, an awareness of the structural complexities of each sentence will serve as an important guide to help us control the pace of the reading. The knowledge will direct our understanding of the speech rhythms in the passage as well as the need for pauses at appropriate places. It will assist us in targeting areas of emphasis within the text which we wish to make clear for our audience. Finally, it will assist us in establishing a better sense of communication between the author, our listeners, and us.

Although there are many ways of classifying sentences according to type, we will be concerned only with the simpler ones: declarative, interrogative, imperative, and exclamatory.

We as listeners tend to suspend our attention through a sentence until we know by traditional clues of inflection and pause that the reader or speaker has completed the thought with all its modifications and qualifications. From this it should be clear that the structure and type of a sentence is important to us when we are trying to infuse those ink-on-paper symbols with vitality, meaning and relevance for our listeners.

The most common form, the simple declarative sentence moves in the expected order from a subject, "who," to the verb/action, "did what." With this kind of sentence our minds don't need to hold an idea in suspension while waiting for qualifying phrases and clauses. With declarative sentences there is always a satisfying sense of completion. The sentence is usually brief and conclusive. The simplest of these consist of just two words as the noun + verb combination found in the Bible's shortest verse: "Jesus wept." While this example is exceptional, the effect of short sentences inserted among longer and more complex ones is the same: it provides us with an interval in which to gather our thoughts about previous statements or actions or to focus on a new idea.

Questions, or interrogative sentences as they are formally called, may be either *direct* or *rhetorical*. A direct question will be followed by an answer. This form is usually found in dialogue or drama. The passion story contains just such an exchange when Jesus is questioned by Pilate:

> Pilate went back into the praetorium and summoned Jesus. "Are you the King of the Jews?" he asked him. Jesus answered, "Are you saying this on your own, or have others been telling you about me? (Jn 18:33–34, NAB).

A rhetorical question is one for which no answer is expected. It is often used to introduce a philosophical topic or underscore a point. Sometimes the question itself is unanswerable or the answer is already well known and therefore need not be made. Paul makes use of many such questions in First Corinthians to force his audience into a proper response:

> Do you not know that you are God's temple and that God's Spirit dwells in you? (1 Cor 3:16, RSV).

Many of Paul's rhetorical questions are lead-in sentences to topics he will explore in subsequent writings.

An interesting use of interrogatives is to be found in Job 38, where God poses a long series of questions. God starts many of his questions to Job with "Can you?" or "Did you?" or "Have you?" By their direct interrogation and the use of "you" they seem to demand an answer which Job cannot make.

As the speech progresses the questions become more and more rhetorical and serve as lead-ins for those descriptive declarative sentences in which God demonstrates his power and wisdom. The combination of interrogative and declarative sentences lends interesting variety to the section. It also sets up an alternating rhythm of focus that shifts from Job, to whom the questions are addressed, to God, who asks the questions and who controls all the elements and wild creatures over which Job is powerless. Finally Job can only say:

> I have dealt with great things that I do not understand; things too wonderful for me, which I cannot know (Job 42:3, NAB).

An interrogative sentence implies a pause to enable the listeners to formulate at least a mental answer, so it also has an effect on the pace of the reading.

A commanding, or imperative, sentence cuts directly into the minds of the hearers since it is a command for some action on their part. The Sermon on the Mount is filled with such statements.

> You have learned that they were told, "Love your neighbor, hate your enemy." But what I tell you is this: Love your enemies and pray for your persecutors; only so can you be children of your heavenly Father, . . .(Matt 5:43, New English Bible).

Sometimes the command is directed toward some other agent whose action will directly affect the listeners, as Jesus' command to the Gerasene/Gadarene demons (Mk 5:8).

If you look at three parallel versions of Genesis 1, shown below, as they are recorded in the King James Version, the Torah and The Jerusalem Bible you find some patterns that become useful in the oral reading of these passages.

In the first chapter of each we find an excellent example of the effective use of varying types of grammatical structure. The direct statement "God said" introduces each new episode. What God said is then expressed in the imperative/command form: "Let." The sentences involving the actions of creation become more complex in structure with lots of qualifying clauses and phrases as the work of creation itself becomes more complex. But each action is concluded with the simple statement, "And so it was," or some variation of this wording. Moreover, each day is concluded with an identical declarative sentence.

King James	*Torah*	*Jerusalem Bible*
In the beginning God created the heavens and the earth.	When God began to create the heaven and the earth—the	In the beginning God created the heavens and the earth.
And the earth was without form, and void; and darkness	earth being unformed and void, with darkness over the	Now the earth was a formless void, there was darkness over
was upon the face of the deep.	deep and a wind from god sweeping	the deep, and God's spirit hovered over the water.
And the Spirit of God moved upon the face of the waters. And God said, Let there be light: and there was light	over the water— God said, "Let there be light"; and there was light.	God said, "Let there be light," and there was light.
And God saw the light that it was good: and God divided the light from the darkness. And God called the light Day, and the darkness he called Night. And the evening and the morning were the first day.	God saw that the light was good, and God separated the light from the darkness. God called the light Day, and the darkness He called Night. And there was evening and there was morning, a first day.	God saw that the light was good, and God divided light from darkness. God called the light "day," and the darkness he called "night." Evening and morning came: the first day

The *word order* of sentences is also important. Whatever is given to us first in a sentence we tend to put foremost in our minds. When the opening word or words serve to connect two related ideas or events as in "on the other hand" or "at a later time," we respond by holding the previous thought suspended in our attention until its counterpart has been completed. The opening sentence of Genesis has this suspended effect, whether the translator has chosen to say, "In the beginning," as is true of most Christian versions, or "When God began," with which the modern Torah opens. In all versions, an interesting shift in word order comes at the climax of God's work with only very slight variations on the following:

> God created man in the image of Himself, in the image of God He created him; (created He him) male and female He created them (created He them)

Here the shift in word order intensifies the act of creating humankind.

Exclamations often cause the interpreter some discomfort. The appearance of an exclamation point seems to indicate some special, emotionally charged break in the continuity of thought. However, the exclamation point, like most punctuation, is simply a signal to our eye. It contributes to the sense or significance of the preceding word or words. And since exclamations are frequently not complete sentences, it serves to identify them as interjections within the complete thought. They usually do indicate a more intense emotion, but they are simple to handle if we look at them as a contribution to, or commentary on, whatever has preceded or, more frequently, what is about to follow rather than considering them as important in themselves. Exclamation points were quite fashionable in previous centuries when some of the translations were made, just as dashes and semicolons seem to be in vogue today. However, the New English Bible, published in 1970, makes frequent use of exclamation points! It is best to let the sense and emotional level of the selection dictate whether the exclamation should stand as a high point by itself or whether, as is more usual, the statement should be blended into the material that follows.

Sentence Length

Obviously the length of a sentence tells us very little in itself. But it is affected by three literary elements,

1. the complexity of the thought being expressed,
2. the way the thought is divided into speech phrases,
3. the number of stressed syllables needed to provide clarity of that thought.

A rhythm of thought and a rhythm of sound flow are established when long, complex sentences alternate with, or are interspersed by, short direct sentences. For our purpose, the numbers of words and syllables in a sentence, and the division of sentences into smaller image/thought units, provide the key to the rate of reading which is required, and to the breath control needed to manage each segment.

One way to discover the rhythms of a passage is to count the numbers of words, then the numbers of syllables in each sentence. This does not mean that we are expected to count every word and syllable in every sentence in the two scriptures before we can communicate the Bible to an audience. It does mean that, by counting words-and-syllables-per-sentence in the passage we are to read, we will have a clearer idea of what sort of speech rhythm that selection requires from us in performance. The practice of numbering words/syllables is simply a way to graphically represent sentence *length* as we look at the relationship between sentence *parts*. It is usually enough to note the relative length or brevity of sentences, although, if you are a serious student of literary style, it is interesting to observe the patterns that develop within a well-written selection.

As we said earlier, one of the reasons why we count sentences and words and syllables is to try to determine the overall rhythm of the selection. If you count the total numbers of sentences and words in each version of the creation story in Genesis, you learn that the Torah uses forty-two sentences containing 867 words, the thirty-three sentences in King James use 796 words, and The Jerusalem Bible's forty-five sentences total 792 words.

The thirty-three sentences of the King James version vary in length from six to fifty-six words. The repeated sentence enumerating the days uses just ten words. There is no clearly discernible pattern for sentence lengths, but length tends to increase as the acts of creation progress and become more complex. The Torah's forty-two sentences range from four to fifty-four words. The lengths of the sentences reflect a pattern of organization alternating from long to short. Reading the account of the fifth day of creation will show you what we mean.

In Genesis we are carried through relatively long sentences in which God expresses his idea for the next stage, then things are halted for the simple statement of the actualization of that idea with "And so it was." This is followed by a longer sentence, balanced into two parallel clauses which name the parts to be created. Then we read a shorter statement of God's satisfaction in the realization. This pattern of alternating between long and short sentences is repeated fairly consistently throughout the creation story and sets up a rhythm of suspension and steadying which can be very helpful in clarifying the story's organization and progression. Such a pattern also helps to develop the significant relationship between the various parts and the whole act of creation.

The numbers of words and syllables used create the distinctive rhythms of the three versions. Thus the King James version, because of its continuing use of the connective "and," gives the reader a sweeping, flowing, cumulative feeling as creation progresses. We are caught up in the vastness of the whole accomplishment. The constructions in The Torah and the Jerusalem Bible distinguish more clearly between each step of the creation so that the divine order and interdependence of all created things seem more apparent.

This is a very brief and fragmentary look at sentence length and organization. And as we have already said, this analysis is not intended to imply that we must count every syllable of every sentence before we read from the Bible. It is merely intended to point out means of using attributes already present in each translation by which we can determine something about the nature of the speech rhythms inherent in each. And these rhythms often help us to choose the best translation for our particular audience.

Notes

1. In any close literary analysis of the Bible one is immediately confronted with the problem of multiple translations and editing styles. For our discus-

sions we have selected from among several of these texts. In each case we have tried to choose the one which best illustrates the point under discussion. You are invited to do some comparison, perhaps by examining the eight translations which appear side by side in the Parallel Gospel, to see the ways word choices vary from one translation to the other.

2. The "because you are special" phrase is still very much with us in today's advertising messages and campaigns—an indication that this persuasive device still works.

3. These headings, which appear here in quotation marks, are to be found in the New Revised Standard Version.

5

Narratives

Sometimes it is difficult for us to think about the literature of the Bible in terms of "prose," or "poetry" or "drama." And it is really not necessary for us to do so. Some books, such as Genesis, Exodus, Samuel, and Chronicles may be better thought of as history. Others, such as the story of David or of Elias, or the whole of the book of Kings, are really biographies. But both of these forms—history and biography—are really types of a single literary form called narrative. There are some basic differences between the organization of the material in the two, but the terms "history" and "biography" are really no more than practical working classifications for the subject matter of the books. And when we judge the two forms by their purposes, they are primarily informational.

To a degree, both history and biography are part of the world of myth. They are retellings of events and lives from the past, which is the material of folktales. They resemble folklore in that both forms are often based on facts, but with the content arranged in imaginative story form, similar to fiction. So we as lectors must pay close attention to both the factual and to the mythic elements which are present in each selection.

To begin to understand the characteristics of narrative writing in general and the problems that are inherent in reading this form aloud, let's start with what narratives are.

A *narrative* tells a story. It tells what happened to someone, some-where, at some time. It may tell us how and why the story came to be; it may be true or fictional or a combination of both. The narrative/story form is probably as old as humankind. It is popular because it re-creates an experience so completely that the listeners share in it. But, while we are busy trying to make these narratives come alive, biblical scholars and theologians have been busy trying to kill the vitality of the tales with the idea that some of the stories may be mythic in nature. Elizabeth Cook writes that, in their scholarly demythologizing zeal "the truth of Biblical fantasy does not seem to interest them. . . . Before very long it will be the work of teachers of literature to tell the stories of the Old Testament, and perhaps the New as well—if it is not already theirs."[1]

Our concern is not with establishing the factual or mythic bases of the stories contained in the Bible. Instead we will look at how the authors—whoever they may have been—chose to handle the elements of what happened to whom, where, when, how, and why.

As we have said, most of the narratives in the Bible have many of the characteristics of folklore. They were usually *orally transmitted*, so many of the words and rhythmic elements have the literary qualities of poetry. These are devices which helped the teller remember the events of the story. They are vestiges of the storytelling tradition with which the stories began. Sometimes there are *quite different versions* of the same story, often with a lot of very apparent discrepancies. The contrasting versions of the creation, the great flood, the differing accounts of the fall of Adam and Eve, are examples that may come to your mind. The gospel writers chose different elements to describe the birth of Jesus. They chose different scenes and events to describe his passion, death, and resurrection. The facts of birth and death are present in all of the gospels but the amount and arrangement of the details varies widely from one writer to another.

Folklore always exhibits these discrepancies. The teller selects the tale he wishes to relate. He then adapts the facts of the story to fit the needs or interests of a particular audience. So folktales often reflect local or national characteristics as well. Changes of emphasis in the choice of details used will vary with the political climate of the time. The oral tradition assumed that the storyteller had a strong sense of the needs of his audience and what their responses would be, since he usually lived in the middle of the society for whom the story was being told. The problems of that community were as acutely present to him as they were to his audience.

There are some real problems for us as modern-day storytellers of these biblical narratives. First, the stories are so familiar to us and to our audiences that we are often tempted to ignore the importance of our roles as community storytellers. We are apt to just read the words and neglect to share the *experience* with our hearers. The important words here are *share* the *experience* of the story. In order to share an experience we need to relive it actively ourselves. We need to become involved in what happened to the people in the story as nearly as we can, given a separation of thousands of years, projecting back in time, in order to effectively involve our listeners of today. This is a hard job. It requires control and response of both our voice and our body. It involves active mental concentration, and often a bit of impersonation as well. And both of these elements relate to *directness*.

We touched on the importance of focus and projection in our discussion of the use of the voice in interpretation. We also discussed muscle tone and empathy as they relate to the use of the body. All of these elements are a part of that principle of *directness*. But, directness is first of all a mental matter. We must think both to our audiences and with them.

We begin with the stimulus we get from the printed page as we translate the symbols into sounds, ideas, and emotions. We prepare the selection carefully, so that we know how every part fits into the design of the story.

Don't get the idea that you have to know the work completely. The truth is that we *never* know a work of good literature completely. One of the delights of good writing is that there is always more to discover with subsequent reading. What we are saying is that, as lectors, we need to know the work as well as we can *right now*, where we are in our growing appreciation of the Bible both as inspiration and as literature. Once we have prepared as thoroughly as we can, we then turn our attention out to the audience, using all of our vocal and physical techniques to reach their minds and emotions.

We do not make them come to us. We go to them.

We do this in everyday life. You have had the experience of attempting to tell someone a funny or serious incident, an occasion which moved you so much that you wanted your listeners to know every detail so they could experience the same emotions you felt. We all have done it. And sometimes we find ourselves falling short, saying finally, "I guess you had to have been there." But if you recall the feel-

ings associated with your retelling, you remember that you concentrated on making the chain of events as vivid as possible. Your body and
your voice reflected the tensions which colored the experience. We
almost unconsciously use every technique to hold our listeners' attention. We suggest the places, the people involved, the steps leading to
the crucial, climactic event, and the impact of the climax itself.

Too often readers of biblical and religious literature surround
themselves with such a mist of theological footnotes that the stories
never come to life. And the more familiar the story, the more effort it
seems to require to make it vivid enough to achieve its full purpose. A
truly good reading may provide the listener with his first *real* experience of what the story says. Our task is more important today than
ever before. But how can we do it? To do our job effectively we must
take our cue from the narrator/storytellers and become re-creators of
the experience.[2]

Since we know how to read aloud, and we are responsive to God's
word and world, we are already on our way. We have all the necessary
tools to make the Bible live.

Point of View

Every narrative has a narrator. Like the storyteller, he selects and
arranges details for their effect on an audience. The presence of the
narrator determines what literary scholars call *point of view*. The term
has been defined as the physical and psychological position the narrator takes in relation to the action, the characters, and the plot. Put
another way, point of view tells us where the narrator stands to view
the people and events of the story. Although the term point of view is
a modern one the technique itself is ancient. Writers have for centuries made point of view significant in its application. And the concept is extremely useful to anyone reading biblical narratives.

Let's be clear about one thing: the narrator is not the original and
actual author. The narrator is the writer's mouthpiece, the mega-
phone/microphone through whom she or he tells the story. The
degree of characterization or personality of the narrator—as supplied
by the author—may range all the way from the first-person narrator,
who is involved as a major and central figure in the plot, to an almost
detached third-person narrator, who simply reports what may be seen

and heard. The account of the Israelites' escape from Egypt, including the parting of the Red Sea and the destruction of Pharaoh's army is an example of this type. Between these two extremes there are innumerable variations. But it is impossible for a first-person narrator to know the thoughts of any other character besides his own.

A third-person narrator, one who uses "he," "she," or "it," may be said to be *omniscient*, knowing everything that everyone is thinking as well as what everyone is doing. Narrators may tell us of events which they could not possibly have witnessed within the framework of the story. The narrator of many of the events in the Christian scripture does just this. The narrator in Luke's gospel, telling of the visit to the temple when Jesus was twelve, writes of Mary that she "kept all these things in her heart." He knows something no person except Mary could know. In other cases a narrator may limit omniscience to only one or perhaps two of the characters. The narrator may have a distinct personality or may simply be "someone" telling the story.

At first glance it would seem that most of the narrators in the Bible are completely trustworthy. After all, they are bringing us the Word of God. But Wayne Booth, in his book *The Rhetoric of Fiction*, raises an interesting question about the very first narrator in the Book. We know that narrators can be omniscient, telling us what the people in a story are thinking as well as what they are doing. But Booth's question is: Before there was anything in the cosmos, before the creation of the world and intelligence in the world—how does the narrator know what God was thinking?[3] The fact is that we do accept that the narrator knows what was in God's mind, just as we accept the other narrators in the Bible. Booth points out that we accept the validity of many narrators, as we accept the statements about God's thoughts, because ". . . It is information that we must accept without question if we are to grasp the story that is to follow."[4] We assume, because of their association with the ruling force, the creative base for everything that lives, these narrators are speaking the complete truth.

We often assume that most of the narrators in the two scriptures are objective third-person storytellers. But, on closer examination, we find a wide variety of narrative points of view. The sixth chapter of Isaiah presents us with a first-person narrator as the prophet tells us of his call: "Then I heard the Lord saying, 'Whom shall I send? Who will go for me?' And I answered, 'Here am I; send me'" (Isa 6:8–9 New

English Bible). The narrator in the book of Kings moves in and out of the story. At times he lets an episode complete itself before making specific comments about either the event or the characters involved or both. The narrator in the story of Joseph often seems to disappear, obliterated by the quick succession of events in the story and by his skill in keeping our attention focused on Joseph and his family. Nevertheless, he does tell us the secret thoughts and fears and ambitions in the minds of the characters. He is even omniscient in his knowledge of Yahweh's care and commendation of Joseph throughout his career.

The parables of the Christian scripture offer a particularly interesting study in point of view. As we read the gospels it is quite clear that the main events of Jesus' life can be chronicled with strikingly different effects by different writers. Although Matthew, Mark, Luke, and John are all strongly sympathetic to Jesus, we need only compare the Sermon on the Mount as told by Matthew and as told by Luke to become aware that the purpose of the retelling, the memory of what was important, and the evaluation of details differ sharply between the two accounts. John, too, often turns the narrative to serve the points he wishes to make. Read his story of Judas at the last supper. John tells us that "Satan entered into him," a detail only John reports and a detail that only an omniscient narrator could know. This is not to say that the recorded memories of the gospel writers are wrong. We are saying, rather, that a narrative always depends upon who wrote it, what narrative voice was chosen to speak and out of what environment.[5]

Action and Plot

The action in biblical narratives is the basis for their organization. It must be remembered that the Hebrews saw life in terms of conduct. That is, they judged both individuals and societies in terms of actions. What a man did brought God's immediately apparent approval or God's rebuke and punishment.

There is a great deal of physical activity in the biblical narratives, although it is never elaborately described. The three-days' journey of Abraham and Isaac to the land of Moriah is told in three sentences. Other activity is often stated as starkly as in the story of Joseph where the writer simply says: "His brothers went to pasture their father's flocks at Shechem," followed by "He [his father] sent him from the valley of Hebron and Joseph arrived at Shechem" (Gen 37:12–15, The Jerusalem Bible). This starkness of detail is not limited to the Hebrew scripture. Many of the accounts of Jesus' activities are characterized by the same condensation of both time and activity. For example, Mark writes of Jesus' baptism at the Jordan (Mk 1:9–11). We are told that the heavens opened and the Spirit descended upon him in the form of a dove and that "a voice came from heaven" proclaiming Jesus as the Son of God. Verse 12 begins:

> Immediately afterwards the Spirit drove him out into the wilderness and he remained there for forty days, and was tempted by Satan. He was with the wild beasts, and the angels looked after him (Mk 1:12–13, The Jerusalem Bible).

The literary term for this bridging of days and weeks is *summary*; time is speeded up to get to the important business of the narrative. When reading highly compressed passages such as these, we must fill out and complete the details within our own minds in order to preserve the organization of the action, since those details are essential to the plot. Only by seeing the total picture clearly will we be able to convey it to our audiences.

Crisis and Climax

In literature the terms *crisis* and *climax* are used to describe the high points of emotional or intellectual intensity in a series of events. *Climax* is used to describe the peak moment, while *crisis* is used to describe the steps of intensity that lead to that peak moment. Crisis points in a story are usually marked as those places at which future possibilities of action are limited or redirected. Each succeeding crisis limits choices for the central characters until only the moment of climax remains. So the *climax* of *action* is built up to by an accumulation of key events, events which must be emphasized to our listeners. There is also a *climax of plot*, or high point in the development of human relationships. Often the climax of action and the climax of plot occur together or in close sequence. Luke's narrative of the birth of Jesus shows such a progression. It begins with the priest Zechariah and the announcement that his wife, Elizabeth, will conceive and bear a son who shall be named John. This news is followed by the angelic annunciation to Mary that she will bear a son who shall be called Jesus. Elizabeth visits Mary; John is born, and Zechariah, his voice returned, "was filled with the Holy Spirit and spoke" a prophecy of John's task preparing the way for the messiah. The climactic point arrives with the birth of Jesus. The resolution of the story comes with the appearance of the angels and the shepherds' journey to see the child. Each event builds on the last to reach the climax—the birth of the savior.

Some narratives focus on the development of a single character. In these the climax is that point at which the character reaches his highest point of development, the point toward which the plot and action have been moving him. In extended narratives, such as the story of Joseph or the account of the trial and crucifixion of Jesus, each step in the overall organization has its own series of crises and climaxes, and they occur in rapid succession.

There is always a building up of tension and intensity within the story. Sometimes, in the minor crises, the tension is very slight but it is always present. But all too often familiarity with the narrative tempts us as interpreters to assume that this increase in tension will emerge without our help. If the plot—often the essential comment on humanity's relationship with God—is to carry impact, we must allow our physical responses to help us. Look back again at the discussions of empathy and muscle tone in chapter 2, since they are particularly applicable here.

In almost every biblical story the narrator reports the climax of action and frequently the end of the plot as well. In the parable of the Prodigal Son, for instance (Lk 15:11–32), it is the narrator who tells us of the return of the son. We must identify with the father's joy at seeing him in order that the welcome and celebration will ring true. We must visualize the arrival and let both body and voice express the motivation for the father's greeting speech. Empathy is particularly important here.

How would you feel in that situation? How do the muscles of your chest, back, legs, even your feet feel when you know joy? We must always ask questions like this and then let our bodies respond to the kinetic and kinesthetic imagery that is present.

Time and Place

We have said that a narrative tells what happened to whom and sometimes where, when, why, and how. "Where" and "when" the action takes place may or may not be important. In biblical stories, however, time progression almost always takes the form of a simple, straight-ahead chronology within individual episodes. Perhaps part of the reason for this is the ancient Hebrews' concept of history, especially the history of the race and its inseparable religious history. *Time matters.* Another part of the reason may be the fact that these stories most certainly came from the oral tradition of the storyteller. Oriental storytellers often see their chief purpose for retelling a familiar story as a good way to remind their listeners of the implications and results of the action rather than to present a full and novel setting for the story. In any case, the sequence of time is basic to the organization of what happened first, then next, and then finally. This progression of events must be made clear to our listeners, so that the experience of the incident or incidents has a beginning, a high point, and a conclusion.

In the prophetic writings of the Bible the narrative units are often drawn from the past history of Israel. They are re-experienced by the prophet in the very recent past, and frequently carry a promise for the future. However, the real telling of the story is immediate and done in terms of present problems and the present audience. The entire book of the Acts of the Apostles is a report of past action as it was seen and heard by Luke. He gives us the time of each event, makes transitions from place to place, identifies the apostles involved, and then records the speech or event. The speeches are put into direct discourse as if they were verbatim transcripts, which may or may not be true. Nevertheless, the fact that the speaker is acting so directly gives them immediacy. The frequent references to the past and to prophecies which have been fulfilled are inserted in the light of present developments. Although place names are often used without any description, the names themselves frequently convey the geographical characteristics of the area.[6]

If you have ever traveled abroad, you are well aware that there is a major difference between being at home and being in a foreign country. As you can imagine, the feeling is compounded if you are in exile. Even trips within your own country show a marked geographic and psychological difference between a seashore and a desert, between a crowded, busy city and a quiet path in a grove of trees. There is a difference between a hilltop, where the countryside is visible for miles, and an enclosed, fertile, protected valley. For the people of Israel these differences were compounded by their dependence upon nature for food and clothing as well as shelter—a dependence most of us will never know. But for the Israelites the seasons and the locations had great effect on both action and plot.

Houses and dwellings are not often described except to indicate the wealth or position of the owner, which is often implied in his occupation. The only full description of a building in the Hebrew scripture is that of the temple built by Solomon in Jerusalem and, even then, the fact that it is located in Jerusalem is the really important fact. With this in mind, it is obvious that whenever a description is given or an adjective is used, it must receive our careful attention. This is equally true of possessive pronouns. When a man goes down into his own house or a tribe comes to its own land, there is an accompanying feeling of peace and security which is essential to the plot.

Journeys are important in the Bible, and the active, kinetic and muscular, kinesthetic imagery that results from them grows out of the sense of the spirit of a place, as a beginning or an end point for the characters. There was dread, grief, sorrow, and a great weariness that accompanied the Israelites on the journey into exile, but the feelings were quite different on the return journey.

Characters

We have said that the basis for organization within most biblical narratives is the action. This action may involve Yahweh's appearance at the moment of climax, speaking directly to the others involved in the story, or to earthly creatures or, not infrequently, to the elements or objects such as a stone or a burning bush or a sea which parts at his command. The plot, however, involves changes in human relationships, either with other human beings or with Yahweh. And thus we come to some considerations of character.

There are always at least two ways of presenting a story. The narrator may comment on events and individuals. That is, he may tell us about them, or he may show us, by allowing them to speak for themselves. When they do speak for themselves it is often that narrator's purpose to allow them to disclose important insights into their character.[7] However, most of the information we need about the characters in biblical literature is given directly by the narrator of the story. Sometimes, as in the case of Reuben who intended to save Joseph from his brothers, the narrator tells us what is in the character's mind:

> Reuben said to them, 'Shed no blood; throw him into this pit here in the wilderness, but lay no hand on him'—*that he might rescue him out of their hand and restore him to his father* (Gen 37:22, NRSV, emphasis added).

More frequently, however, the actions speak for themselves.

We learn about a character in a piece of literature by noting what he says about himself and what others, including the narrator, say about him. He also reveals himself in his actions and his responses to the actions of others. There are numerous instances of this throughout both scriptures.

The most important aspect of a biblical character is his inner response pattern. This pattern grows out of his attitudes toward himself and others, toward his environment, and toward actions performed by himself and by others. These dictate his responses and his consequent actions. His exterior qualities—age, sex, position in society, physical health, and so forth, strongly influence his inner qualities—his sense of values, and thus his degree of psychological and emotional tension in a given set of circumstances. The character is complete only when the interior and exterior qualities are logically related.

In order to become involved in the action and the plot of a story, our listeners must be aware of the kind of person speaking or acting. We must use both voice and body to suggest the state of mind, in the broadest sense, of the character himself. When the narrator creates a scene and peoples it with characters who speak or whose thoughts he knows and reveals, we must reflect all we are given of each character's responses.

This is not to say that we must become actors, but neither are we simply reporters who are indifferent to the events of the story. We will use empathy, muscle tone, and posture to suggest strength or fear or great sorrow or joy. These emotions are also reflected in pace, rhythm, and general tone of vocal communication. As you are already aware, you can often decode the emotional import of a conversation even when the words are not heard. By the same token, you cannot expect an audience to believe the words they are hearing if you look and sound detached, unmoved and uninterested. In order for the impact of the Bible to come through, you must make it come alive, you must make it immediate. You *must share the experience* with them, letting them feel through your words and actions what the people of the story are feeling "right now."

Our listeners may already be familiar with the action but they may not as yet have shared the implications of the changes in human relationships which form the plot of the story and which carry the true impact of the narrative.

Stories have always had an enormous appeal. They are extremely effective devices for illustrating and clarifying whatever may lie slightly beyond the grasp of our finite minds. We can understand by analogy and parable what we cannot understand in any other way when the telling is vivid and allows us to relate it to our own lives in a personal, experiential way. Consequently, if we attempt to underplay the story elements in a narrative in the hope of making it more relevant to a modern audience, we are, in fact, defeating our own purpose. The stories charmed us as children, and when they are well and properly re-created, they hold our interest and bring us new insights as adults. Their very familiarity helps to establish a sense of continuity we all so desperately need today.

Notes

1. Elizabeth Cook's comments appear in her book *The Ordinary and the Fabulous* (Cambridge University Press: Cambridge, England, 1969), pp. 37–38.

2. For more on biblical storytelling see Tom Boomershine's book on the subject, *Story Journey* (Nashville, TN: Abingdon Press, 1988).

3. Wayne C. Booth, *The Rhetoric of Fiction* (Chicago, IL: University of Chicago Press, 1967).

4. Booth, op.cit. p. 3 ff.

5. In his study of the parables of Jesus, a voice in the study of Redaction Criticism, Joachim Jeramias, points out that the parables as they appear in the gospels often seem to be contradictory. Jeramias' point is that the same story,

told to two different audiences, may be altered to make different philosophical or moral points. The determinant is the type of audience and that audience's needs. Joachim Jeramias, *The Parables of Jesus*, Second Revised Edition (New York: Charles Scribner's Sons, 1972), pp.31-42.

6. In Numbers 21:14 we read that "the Lord speaks of Vaheb," which is defined as meaning "watershed." Five verses later "From there they moved on to Beer: this is the waterhole where the Lord said to Moses. . . ." Here the place name is defined in the text—"Beer" means "water-hole." In other narratives a place is named because of its religious significance. The fifth chapter of Joshua tells of the Israelites' entry into the promised land. In verse 9, "The Lord then said to Joshua, 'Today I have rolled away from you the reproaches of the Egyptians.' Therefore the place is called Gilgal to this very day" (New English Bible). A footnote explains that "Gilgal" means "Rolling Stones." The genius or spirit of the place was important to the Hebrew mind. Historical significance, of the nation as it developed or within the narrator's or character's own lineage, was more important than the outward features of the place.

7. The idea of "telling" and "showing" as a means for narrating a story comes from Booth's *The Rhetoric of Fiction* (Chicago, IL: University of Chicago Press, 1967.), Chap. 1 passim.

6

Narrative in the
Hebrew Scriptures

The literature of the Hebrew scriptures makes some heavy demands on us as liturgists. The first of these comes from the variety of literary types found there. This account of the history of the children of Israel contains almost every form of literature we know. A real problem for lectors today is the complexity of references—the names, places, relationships—which accompany the stories. And we often get a sense that several people are telling the tale, as in the story of David in 1 and 2 Samuel. All of these details require our attention. Then we must remember that the Hebrew scripture spans centuries of Jewish history, and many long-forgotten storytellers carried the stories in their minds, passing them down from one generation to the next, until the accounts could be set down on parchment.

As we have said, the Hebrew storyteller often presented his story directly to his audience. Two factors entered into his method of telling. The first was that few members of his audience could read, so the impact of the story had to be made quickly since the storyteller's art exists "right now" for his audience[1]. Listeners could not stop and rethink a section which was not clear on the first hearing. A second factor was that Hebrew syntax lent itself well to the condensed storytelling form. It has been a great convenience to our contemporary Sunday ritual that we have come to think of Hebrew scripture as a series of separate short episodes. But we have done a great disservice to the literature of that scripture by ignoring—for our own liturgical expedience—the fact that these stories are a series of continued and interestingly structured chronicles.

Biblical scholars tend to divide the writings of the Hebrew scriptures into two periods, the classical or pre-exilic and the romantic, post-exilic. Important as such a division is for categorizing the material historically, it is really not much help to us when we read the stories in a worship service. For one thing, these periods are not at all clear-cut and distinct. Like all "movements" in literature, changes take place slowly and there is a lot of overlapping in the writing style and literary characteristics of the two periods. So it is more helpful for us to examine a selection, not from its historical category, but from the standpoint of its individual organization. We need to be aware of the narrative writing techniques the individual selection demonstrates, as well as of the other details and stylistic variations that will require our attention. It goes without saying that we do this with an understanding that the Hebrew scripture is basically the history of a nation, and that the narrative/story form is used as a means of historical recollection as well as storyteller involvement.

There are three types of history to be found throughout the Bible. Some of the history is descriptive; it tells what took place, and where. This latter type is much less concerned with a "message" than are the other two. There are exceptions, of course, but their purpose is just disclosure of events. There is didactic history which points out a lesson or teaches an historic truth. Much of the 2 Kings serves just this purpose. And there is the more sophisticated "scientific" history, which emphasizes cause and effect. This last form tends to overlap the other two types regularly. So an understanding of the purpose of the story and the intended receivers will influence our choices of narrator style, character involvement, and method of organization. All of these elements are important to us as liturgists/lectors.

Since much of the history found in Hebrew scripture is written in the form of biography, we need to pay particular attention to the aspects of character and character analysis we have already discussed. Our listeners must be made aware that the subject of the story is being used as a *symbol*. But for us, while we are dealing with the symbol, the *individual* must emerge in all his strength or holiness or anger or power, just as these qualities emerged during that person's lifetime.

There are occasions when there is more heroism than true history in some of the stories. A case in point is the book of Daniel. But such heroism had its purpose then, just as it has in all of the epics and sagas which have emerged since. In the case of Daniel, the story served to encourage the nation at the beginning of a long and difficult period of war and conflict. The Israelites needed a hero; the character of Daniel was an ideal choice.

Characters

As with all narrative, the characters in the Hebrew scripture stories reveal themselves to us in two ways. They reveal their personality and character through their words. So we must often rely on the voice of the narrator to report, not only what the characters said, but also the tone and the thoughts and motives which lay behind the person's speech. Of course, characters reveal themselves to us through their actions as well—actions which the narrator reports. These reports are usually made without comment on motivation beyond our own general assumptions. And these, in turn, are based on the situation and the character's general temperament or position as we have observed it. We recall both the speaker's words and the descriptions supplied by the narrator. But in dealing with figures in Hebrew scripture we need to keep in mind that many of the characters' decisions and consequent actions were not mere personal choices. They grew out of the associative power of the Hebrews' linear concept of the past and their limitless concept of their future through Yahweh's continuing presence. God has always been viewed as the strength and ongoing support of both the person and the nation.

In the narratives of the Hebrew scripture we are frequently faced with clearly-defined character "types." The strong are tremendous in their strength, and the weak, the cunning, the wicked, the wise, and the good are all equally true to type. Despite the two-dimensional style, some of these character types provide considerable insight into human nature. We must never be trapped into treating these people as caricatures. Their speech and action is realistic. When a king wishes someone summoned into his presence, he says so. When he punishes a slave, there is neither question nor rationalization.

Because they are pure types, most of the characters of the Hebrew scriptures will not give you much trouble in presenting them. You may need to do a bit of research to acquaint yourself with some of the aspects of ancient law and the importance of family and lineage in order to fully understand the characters' motivations for their actions.

Most of the time, however, you will find that these details exactly fulfill the requirements of each individual's particular position in the story.

There is one truly difficult problem for us as readers of the Hebrew scriptures. How will you handle the voice of God? The same problem will surface in the Christian scripture in those direct discourse passages attributed to Jesus.

We do not know how God sounded when he spoke to the Israelites. We do not know how he looked. He was usually not seen as a person at all. What we do know is the Hebrew and Christian concept of his power and strength and of his constant concern for the good or evil actions of mankind. For example, in the opening chapters of Genesis, God is going about a tremendous task with authority and efficiency. He uses the command form "Let" with the complete assurance that it will be done right now! There is majesty in each speech, but there is no sense of aggressiveness. When we read these passages, we must give them the full dimension they require. And when each episode is completed we must be very sure God's satisfaction and approval is made clear.[2] Much of the Hebrew scriptures shows a judgmental God who is often angry at his people. His anger certainly is clear when he delivers his curse on the serpent:

> Because you did this,
> Banned shall you be from all cattle
> And all wild beasts;
> On your belly you shall crawl
> And dirt shall you eat
> All the days of your life.
> I will put enmity
> Between you and the woman,
> And between your offspring and hers
> They shall strike at your head,
> and you shall strike at their heel. (Gen 3:14–15, The Torah)

Clearly, God's feeling of divine wrath must be suggested through your voice and your body when you read that passage aloud. On the other hand, a different style is needed when we recount the words God spoke to Samuel (1 Sam 3:11–14). He explains his future action to the boy with carefully controlled, reasoned language, concealing his anger against the House of Eli. His all-knowing wisdom when he speaks to Job is partly revealed by the fact that he leaves a lot unsaid that Job wants to hear. God's speeches are full of devastatingly reasonable questions to which Job can give only one answer. We urge you to look closely at the word choices and the overall rhythm of the lines of each speaker in these stories. It will help you communicate the differing attitudes both of God and of the people in the stories.

Understanding of character traits and character types is most important in those sections of the scriptures which are best classified as "short stories." The books of Ruth, Jonah, and Esther are good examples. For instance, in the book of Esther it is vital that we make the audience aware of the incident with Queen Vashti, which puts Esther into a position of influence with the king. Esther's humility contrasts sharply with the pride of both the king and his queen. The differences in the three personalities, coupled with the customs of the era, need to come through to our listeners in order for the impact of the story to be relevant to them. And most of this information comes through the voice of the narrator.

Look at the relatively small amount of dialogue in the first part of the story. There are many things which need to be explained to us and, apparently, to the audience the storyteller was addressing. It is the narrator who takes us through a period of time rich with Persian manners and customs until the moment when Esther is established as queen. Only then do we encounter dialogue, as she pleads with Ahasuerus. And, while the king's proclamations are put into direct discourse, dialogue does not emerge again until Haman has his ill-fated interview. The narrator controls the flow of the story. He only presents the characters "in scene" when there is a need to *show* the speakers through one-to-one conversation.[3]

The book of Ruth has been called a story without a villain. It is often described as an idyll of love and domestic happiness. It is for this reason, perhaps, that the characters are drawn with much deeper and more human responses than those we find in Esther. The story exhibits a perfect unity of the development and growth of the relationship, first between Ruth and her mother-in-law, Naomi, and then between Ruth and Boaz. And all of the development takes place without the narrator's help. There is no need. The motives are clear and perfectly understandable within the context of the laws and customs under which the people lived.

In our discussion of time and place we mentioned the importance of one's own land and people. Importance of land and people is very much at the heart of the story of Ruth. It adds strong undertones of loneliness and courage as Ruth follows the harvesters to glean the grain. The style of writing in the story is simple, yet it moves with a kind of serene dignity. The sentences are relatively long and have an easy, flowing rhythm, fitting the nature of the story. There is a great deal of dialogue which allows the characters to reveal their thoughts and attitudes more clearly than if the narrator simply reported what they said or thought. In re-creating the story we must take care that the attitudes of the central characters toward each other are strongly suggested as the material is read aloud. The action develops because of the kind of relationship these people have with one another. If these relationships are not made abundantly clear to an audience, the story becomes just another sentimental tale with a happy ending. We must believe in these people and in their gentle tolerance and devotion. They speak directly and intimately to each other and we must make our listeners aware of this as we read.

Yet another approach is required when we tell of God's attitude toward the opinionated and self-righteous Jonah. Jonah provides one of several examples of humor in Hebrew scripture. Human like the rest of us, he shrinks from the call he receives from God. Then he tries to outwit God. God plays the game with him and Jonah loses every hand! It is certainly not meant to be authentic history; it is a satiric lesson in the form of an allegory. There are such delightful touches as, "They [the sailors] already knew that he was trying to escape from the LORD, for he had told them so" (1:10–11, The New English Bible). And when we remember that he had not told them his business, or his country, we are amused at the idea of Jonah confiding his plight to a group of rough sailors. Later, after Jonah's repentance inside the fish, we hear that "the LORD spoke to the fish and it spewed Jonah out on dry land" (2:10, NEB). What charming playfulness in the idea of the great and mighty God speaking with the fish about the man, Jonah!

And finally there is the picture of Jonah, pouting and angry, sitting (with his arms crossed, one is sure) outside the city of Nineveh, demanding its destruction. Then it is that the mighty God who caused the turmoil in the sea first causes a vine to grow to shade Jonah, then sends a worm to take it away. All of this effort just to teach Jonah a lesson, which God could have done with one stroke! The reason for the whole game between God and Jonah is clear: God understands and tolerates the Jonahs among us.

The proportion between dialogue and narrative is almost exactly balanced in the story of Jonah. And it is interesting to contrast God's choice of words and the simplicity of the syntax he uses with Jonah when it is compared with some of the utterances he makes in more crucial and historic situations elsewhere in Hebrew scripture. God's charge to Jonah is simple and direct: "Go to the great city of Nineveh, go now and denounce it, for its wickedness stares me in the face" (1:2, NEB).[4]

Climax of Plot and Action

The brevity and immediacy of the stories of which we have spoken produce an effect on the speed and impact of the climaxes within episodes or the major climax of an extended story. In the story of Joseph, for example, it is extremely difficult to pinpoint the major climax of the plot. In part, at least, this is the result of the interweaving of the elements of family history and the nature of the various people who operate in close relationship to Joseph. But we must always remember that, as the story of Joseph and the other heroes unfolds, the central figure grows both in strength and maturity. So the Joseph who confronts his brothers in Genesis, chapter 42, is quite a different person from the young boy who enquired politely for information about them in chapter 37 (vs 16–17). He is reacting differently again when he greets his father in a later chapter. His growth and the authority which has been given him must be evident in his bearing and tone in chapter 42. His deep devotion to his father, as well as his capacity to act in his father's behalf, will affect his thinking, his posture, even his pace of speaking in chapter 46. At the same time, the narrator(s) never let us forget that Yahweh was always with him, and Yahweh made everything he undertook successful.

It is important for us to recall the Hebrew concept of a God who showed his approval or his anger immediately and in this world, rather than storing up a person's good and evil deeds for reckoning in the next. With that concept in mind, it becomes evident that the intervention of Yahweh is really the essential unifying force in the total narrative. Joseph's actions and the subplots and changes in human relationships all result from this divine primary motivation. Thus the *climax* of *action* could well be placed at the point of Joseph's final "promotion" to the post of Governor of Egypt. It should be noted, however, that each episode has its own minor climax of action as Joseph succeeds in each endeavor.

It is interesting to note that after Joseph becomes governor another plot line, which began with his dream and which is concerned with his relationship to God and to his family, becomes important. The climax of plot involves Yahweh's relationship to Joseph. This relationship may be seen in Joseph's interpretation of the dream, an interpretation for which God had given him the knowledge. The rest of the story is the *fulfillment* of that prophetic dream. The climax of the relationship between Joseph and his family comes in the ultimate test: the hidden goblet, the demand that Benjamin remain as Joseph's slave, and the brothers' resultant actions which give Joseph the answer he has been seeking throughout the years. This new relationship is fully revealed and solidified in chapter 50. So each episode touching on the family has its own minor climax of plot. Character development parallels the dual development of plot.

Narrative Style

The story of Noah and the flood presents some interesting problems for us to examine. Scholars agree that any version of the Noah story is a composite narrative. And this fact that the story does come to us as the work of multiple authors may account, at least in part, for some of the contradictions from one part of the story to another. This complication, also, has some bearing on the differences in style to be found within any single translation. It is this diversity of style which is important to us as lectors. We must make full use of the stylistic variety within the story without losing the unity, the sequence of events.

The actual story of the flood begins in Genesis 6:5. The introduction is more complex than many of the sections of the Hebrew scripture, despite its compactness and brevity. We are told (Gen. 6:5–7) of

God's sorrow at man's wickedness and that God even regrets his magnificent act of creation. This opening is difficult. It requires a balance of sorrow and annoyance which must motivate all the rest of the action. Then (vs 8) we are introduced to Noah. We are not told why he had "found favor with the Lord," but within the context of the passage it is evident that he is a good and righteous man and must therefore be spared from destruction. The first mention of Noah is followed by the statement that this is his story. We are then told of his goodness and of his three sons, Shem, Ham, and Japheth. In the space of twelve verses we are given God's motivation, Noah's qualifications for survival, and an introduction to his sons, who will figure prominently in those sequences which follow the covenant and the flood. This requirement that we hold a great deal of material in balance is part of our problem as lectors. We must keep the audience aware of three things: the motivations for the destruction of the earth, Noah's qualifications for the preservation of all animal life, and the progressive stages of the flood itself. As we said earlier, even when we are asked to read only a portion of the story, we must always keep the *whole narrative picture* in mind. And the whole story does read like the script for a film. Only by keeping the total picture in our hearers' minds can we help hold together the various parts of the narrative.

We begin the description of the flood with the narrator's statement that the earth was corrupt. This observation is followed by the statement that God had seen the problem; he observed that "all flesh had corrupted its ways upon the earth" (vs 12, The Torah). It is followed by God's explanation to Noah of his intention. Then come the specific instructions for the building of the ark: the kind of wood to be used, the height, length and breadth, how it is to finished inside—details hearers of that earlier time would understand and marvel at. There follows the promise of a covenant. Clearly, a great deal of material is crowded into eight verses. God continues his instructions, and we are told that Noah did all God ordered him to do. Next come the declarations regarding the "clean" and "unclean" creatures which are to comprise the cargo of the ark. Keeping this funnel-like progression, from general statements of condition to the specifics of ark construction to the promise of a covenant, offers us a real challenge to hold all the threads together.

There is a strange interjection here with regard to Noah's age at the time of the flood (Gen 7:6 and 11). The notion that Noah was six hundred years old at the time may tempt some liturgists to adopt a cracked, scratchy voice when reading Noah's lines. Of course, such a choice would be disastrous for the reader and for the listeners. Since both passages are linked to the onset of the event, we must always keep God's action at the forefront, and not be misled by a storyteller's concern with Noah's age.

Noah now has the prescribed numbers of all the creatures of the earth on the ark. He and his wife and his sons and their wives are all aboard. Then we are told, "And Yahweh closed the door behind Noah" (7:16, The Jerusalem Bible). Having the door of the ark closed, we and Noah and all those aboard the ark are ready for the journey.

It is at this point, verse 17, that we find a fascinating shift in the storyteller's style. The graphic description of the rising water is truly cinematic. The structure used here helps us to build the scene from one camera angle to another:

> The flood continued forty days on the earth;
>> and the waters increased and bore up the ark,
>> and it rose high above the earth.
> The water swelled and increased greatly on the earth;
>> and the ark floated on the face of the waters.
> The waters swelled so mightily on the earth
>> that all the high mountains under the whole heaven
>> were covered; the waters swelled above the mountains,
>> covering them fifteen cubits deep. (Gen 7:17–20, NRSV)

It is this demonstration of God's power that brings us to the climax of this section in which everything on earth is destroyed. The destruction is repeated in three successive sentences using the verbs "perished," "died," "destroyed," or "blotted out," depending on the translation, "and only Noah was left and those with him in the ark." The pictorial sequence is complete as we watch the water rising and see the ark sail away, and we are given a long camera view of the mountains as they disappear, with the final "fade-out" shot on the ark.[5]

After the ordeal of the flood, the narrator turns our attention to God's relationship with Noah and the occupants of the ark. This narrator validates the story with exact dates through the first fourteen verses of the eighth chapter. We are given the exact day of the month when the ark came to rest on the mountain of Ararat. We are told that nearly three months later, on the first day of the tenth month, the mountain peaks which were the last to disappear become visible. Not only is this precise time sequence helpful in ordering the events until that moment when Noah can look out and see that the surface of the ground is dry, but also, it lends that narrative credibility which a story of such magnitude requires. We are led to believe this narrator simply because of the chronological precision the story employs. If everything on earth was destroyed, just how the narrator knows is unclear. But we know that the flood is over and the cycles of life have begun again.

The story of the flood itself ends here, but Act Three of the drama/story, the resolution of the whole epic, begins with Genesis 8:15 as the ark is emptied of its cargo. As he had closed the door at the beginning of the journey, so now God tells Noah to disembark. Noah immediately offers sacrifice on a newly built altar and God is pleased with him. God begins the covenant with a promise to himself: "I will never again curse the ground because of humankind, for the inclination of the human heart is evil from youth; nor will I ever again destroy every living creature as I have done."

> As long as the earth endures,
>   seedtime and harvest, cold and heat,
> summer and winter, day and night
>   shall not cease. (NRSV)

Then there is the blessing and the clarification of the covenant between God and "every living thing that is found on the earth" (Gen 9:17, The Jerusalem Bible).

The organization and progression is much simpler in the covenant unit than in the description of the preparation for and duration of the flood. The changes in style are less abrupt and more consistent with the character of Yahweh, who is the only speaker. The narrator, too, returns to a more typical style. The main problem in this last section is in keeping a balance between the passages in which God makes a promise to himself and the more extended promises he makes to every living thing on earth. The real climax to the story comes in the section declaring a new world order and God's assurance which appears in verse 17.

As we noted earlier, our main concern in this narrative is with the nature and point of view of the narrator. The storyteller can become as interesting to an audience as the story itself. In the actual account of the flood there is no discourse, either direct or indirect. So it is the liturgist-as-narrator who must hold in balance all of the various threads of the story.[6] Awareness of the narrator's point of view and analysis of the style and climaxes within the narrative are the keys to success in communicating this, perhaps the best-known story in the Hebrew scriptures.

There are many other narratives in Hebrew scripture, but by and large they have the same general characteristics as those we have discussed. The Hebrew scriptures are a treasure-house, especially for worship leaders who like to create interesting stories and become effective tellers of tales.

Notes

1. Studies of the ancient Hebraic language have revealed no clearcut sequence of tenses. So when a narrator spoke of a past action he often conceived of it as the present. That is to say, he took himself and his listeners back to the event rather than bringing the event up into the light of the present. This stems in part from the concept of permanence deeply rooted in the Hebrew tradition. The Israelites maintained a vigorous, daily awareness of a God whose laws remained unchanging. Nuances of past tense were later sophisticated additions to most languages.

2. It might be well to read (or re-read) James Weldon Johnson's version of "The Creation" in his *God's Trombones*. The language is both vivid and strong yet it is filled with the dignity and splendor of the acts.

3. This is a clear example of Wayne C. Booth's statement, cited earlier, that narrative partakes of both "showing" and "telling," as he described it in his book, *The Rhetoric of Fiction* (Chicago: University of Chicago Press, 1967).

4. Compare this command to the call given to Moses in the third chapter of Exodus. Not only does God appear in a burning bush which is not consumed by the fire but also he speaks with ultimate power, saying: "Come now; I will send you to Pharaoh and you shall bring my people Israel out of Egypt" (vs 10, NEB). These are words to change the world of that day; the words to Jonah will certainly not shape the history of a nation. If carried out they will, at best, brush an annoyance away from the face of God.

5. The unit opens with a mention of the forty days of flood which God had said he would send, but it ends with a statement that the water rose for one-

hundred and fifty days. It can be assumed that the rain continued for forty days and the water kept rising even after that, if one is inclined to be concerned about this discrepancy. However, the references to a specific length of time do serve to bracket the description and can certainly be used to indicate a greater passage of time no matter how that time is reckoned.

6. There is some dialogue at the beginning and the end of these chapters but it is all Yahweh's and it is characterized by sharply contrasting moods.

7

Narrative in the Christian Scriptures

We said that the Hebrew scriptures are really an extended narrative tracing the political and spiritual growth of a nation. The writers used a variety of narrative forms, each stemming from an oral tradition designed to preserve a national heritage. The Christian scriptures trace the history, formation and growth of a new heritage. Here the central interest is not in the development of a nation but in the life and teachings of one man. In the light of contemporary scholarship, it seems clear, as with the Hebrew scriptures, that the accounts of the life of Jesus began with an oral tradition. The story of Jesus is told by those early Jewish Christians from a variety of points of view, each affected by the nature of the narrator and by the time-audience-political environment from which the writing came.[1]

All of the gospels, and most of the book of Acts as well, have some unique characteristics that set them apart from the earlier Hebrew writings. The gospels, too, deal with biography, yet, despite their focus on the life of Jesus, they do not fall so neatly into the typical "biography" mode. Neither are they strictly reminiscences. They are less concerned with delineating a person than in establishing belief in the qualities that person displayed and what that person said. Their energy is directed at proclaiming and publicizing the good news, the "godspell." The writers of these accounts felt that they were in possession of a tremendous fact—the messiah had appeared on earth in mortal form. So their tone is one of announcement, of proclamation of the "good news." The style is simple and geared to specific listening audiences. Though time seems abbreviated, often even compressed, we still get a feeling of order through references to "at that time," "the next day," "on another occasion." Places are usually identified and often explained, since they carry with them many of the same symbolic associations we noted in the narratives of the Hebrew scriptures.

The Gospels

Although the first three gospels appear to be so similar that they are termed "synoptic," that is, "with one eye," there are some noticeable differences in writing style and in the selection of details and episodes. Most contemporary scholars believe that early first-hand accounts of the teaching and sayings of Jesus may have existed within the first churches.[2] There is also a general belief that, with the passing of time, and with the changes wrought by some of the schisms within those early communities, the original accounts have been destroyed or lost. Some of the differences in writing style in those gospels, which remain in our present day Bibles, have usually been attributed to the difference in audiences each of the writers addressed.[3]

As we noted earlier, the first Christians were *Jewish Christians*, and Matthew's gospel seems aimed at them. He shows Jesus as the lineal descendent of David. He details the ways in which Jesus' birth, life and death followed the prophecies of preceding centuries. And he relies heavily on references to the Hebrew scriptures. His proclamation is of God as king of man. And his good news is directed to that part of the oriental world which has come to know, love, and serve that king.

Matthew seems to be the most orderly of the four gospel writers. And he provides the clearest organization, grouping blocks of material around central themes. He supplies necessary connections, especially of time and place. Drawing from accounts such as the gospel of Thomas, he is able to weave the many separate episodes of that book into a connected chronological story. And his primary focus is always on Jesus, the Prince of Israel. The disciples are not developed as individuals, he gives almost no space to Mary or to Joseph, and his account of Jesus' birth is strictly factual.

The gospel generally recognized as the earliest of the three is Mark's. In it Mark speaks repeatedly of the miraculous powers of the messiah. It is generally agreed that Mark was a disciple—may even have been a secretary to—the apostle Peter. As such, Mark often gives us glimpses of the personal experiences, the exchanges between Jesus and his disciples, that were recounted by Peter in his preaching. Mark's accounts are clear and realistic. They emphasize the reactions of the general public and of the crowds which followed Jesus. Through Mark's account we are often able to understand motivations and responses more clearly, despite the rapid movement of the narratives. He frequently uses the present tense to help capture a sense of immediacy for us. On the whole, Mark is more concerned with the deeds of Jesus than with his words.

Most authorities feel Luke gained much of his information through personal inquiry. His narratives are not only orderly but also appear to be concerned with giving exact information. His focus is on the humanity within the divinity of Jesus. And it is in Luke's gospel that we find wonderful touches of the dignity and graciousness of Jesus. Luke gives us the most detailed accounts of Jesus' many journeys and he makes frequent reference to the Holy City. He speaks simply, but his use of Semitic idioms lends symbolism to his account. In fact, it is from Luke that we get the human side of the genealogy of Jesus in contrast to Matthew's "table of descent."

John's gospel has a very different focus from the other three. He goes beyond the fulfillment of prophecy which is the basis for Matthew's work. He is only marginally interested in the miraculous events that are described in Mark. And John extends Jesus' ministry beyond the love for humanity which fills Luke's gospel to proclaim the cosmic significance of Jesus. John's gospel reflects a deeper perception of the mystery of the Logos, the Word, with which John begins his narrative:

> "In the beginning was the Word,
>   and the Word was with God,
>   and the Word was God."

John offers an understanding of Jesus as a figure who existed from the beginning of time, one whose mission was the salvation of the world. He proclaims Jesus as the messiah but also as one whose teaching is aimed at bringing all of humanity to an understanding of the way to a more abundant life. The things Jesus did were signs, says John, and he points out the significance of those action-signs. In contrast to the other gospels, John is much more interested in the function of worship and prayer as exemplified in Jesus' ministry. For some scholars the reason lies in the fact that John's was the last of the gospels to be written, dating well after Jesus' physical presence on earth. John's gospel also seems to have coincided closely with the formalization of the early church.

Narratives and Narrative Types

There are two types of storytelling with which we must work when reading from Christian scripture. There are the teaching stories in which we find Jesus speaking in parables and in conversations with his disciples. And there are the third-person narratives which describe Jesus' travels, his cures and miracles, his sermons and the various occasions and deeds in which he participated. This last group presents somewhat different problems for us as worship leaders. Let us begin, then, with those narrative episodes in which Jesus' words and actions are reported to us by a third-person narrator.

All four writers basically keep themselves and their personalities out of our way. All we really need to know about the speaker and the speaker's attitudes we can learn from the style and selection of details within the passages. However, there are usually some speeches of Jesus to be found in them.[4]

These narrative units are not likely to give us a great deal of difficulty if we maintain the direct discourse within the framework of the episode. But we must be aware of both physical and emotional climaxes within each unit and we must often make abrupt transitions of time and place, from introduction to core to conclusion, in order for the lections to work effectively. Jesus' speeches are usually brief and simple and the situation itself often suggests his attitude at the moment. An example drawn from the miracle of the loaves and fishes as it appears in the New English Bible might prove interesting by way of illustration. It is helpful to observe the differences in what each narrator finds significant in four accounts of the same event as we prepare to read this lection.

Matthew (14:13–21) begins the account with, "When he heard what had happened [the beheading of John the Baptist], Jesus withdrew privately by boat to a lonely place." Matthew seems to indicate that sorrow over the fate of John motivates Jesus' wish to be alone. Mark (6:30–45), on the other hand, attributes his desire for solitude to compassion for his weary disciples. Mark says, "He said to them 'Come with me, by yourselves, to some lonely place where you can rest quietly.'" Luke attributes no motivation to their departure (9:10–18), saying only, "he took them [the apostles] with him and withdrew privately to a town called Bethsaida." Luke makes no mention of the boat referred to by both Matthew and Mark. John begins simply with, "Sometime later Jesus withdrew to the farther shore of the Sea of Galilee (or Tiberias), and a large crowd of people followed." John goes on to tell us that it was near the time of Passover and further identifies Andrew and Philip by name. He has Jesus asking Philip directly where he could buy bread to feed so many people, and John introduces an omniscient narrative voice when he adds, "This he said to test him; Jesus himself knew what he meant to do" (6:6).[5]

Matthew and Mark tend to use longer and more complex sentences in their narrations of the story, whereas Luke and John use shorter sentences of simpler construction. All four mention Jesus' compassion for the crowd and his patience in healing them (or teaching them, as Mark says).

In each gospel the pattern is identical. Each gets directly into the story, which begins with the mention that it was getting late. All four end with the description of the gathering of the fragments of the meal after the crowd was satisfied. John adds a further conclusion that Jesus fled the place because he knew the people would make him their earthly king, but the miracle story itself ends with the account of the gathering of the fragments which filled twelve baskets. Keeping the narrator's intention and direction in mind helps us hold the story together when we are reading for a congregation.

Narrating the Parables

Problems dealing with the "first-person voices" of the scripture become most evident when we are dealing with the teaching parables. The obstacle for us, as liturgists, is similar to the one we discussed in the handling of the speeches of Yahweh in the Hebrew scriptures. We don't know how Jesus' voice sounded any more than we know how he looked. We only have the reports of what he said and did, but nowhere is his voice described.[6] This is a real problem as we approach the task of re-creating Jesus' words. All clues to his voice and his rate of speech must be deduced from his attitudes and his symbolic gestures. An example is that shown when, in his anger he drove the moneychangers from the temple. Here we see flashes both of anger and of great strength. From these, and other, clues we know what kind of a person he was. And we deduce the quality of tone of his voice from the clues we are given. We know he had great wisdom, that he showed great compassion, and patience with those who did not understand. In other places we hear subtle differences between the way Jesus spoke to those individuals who came to ask his help and his tone and choice of words when he preached to the crowds who came to hear him. As we reread some of these passages (aloud!) we become aware of the intimate concern for individuals in the first case and the clarity and simplicity, his forthrightness in the second. There is also a change in his tone when speaking with his disciples, people Jesus knew well, whom he understood perfectly both in their strengths and their weaknesses. These facts give us clues to voice quality and delivery.

Many people have an understandable reticence about trying to pretend to "be Jesus" when they read his words. It is a matter of both taste and reverence. We are reluctant to allow ourselves to identify fully with such a speaker. The tendency, therefore, is to pull back from such identification. The result is that Jesus' words come through as either weak or "customary," the way we've "always heard them read." In either case we are apt to present a picture of a man whose physical presence confirms the "gentle Jesus, meek and mild" image with which he is so often associated. But, as we have seen, the gospel writers describe him as far from meek and often anything but mild. He was a man who learned a trade, worked at it with his father, and even after he began his ministry showed himself to be a vigorous person. His chief concern was with reaching the people around him, touching them with God's love and care. Even when he was tired, as in the unit we discussed above, his compassion for the crowds that followed him made him reach out to them. It is this sense of the stature, physical strength, vigor and concern which must undergird and be the basis for our reading of his words.

A major problem in making Jesus' words come alive is their familiarity. We have heard them quoted and misquoted since we were children. With this heritage at our backs it is tempting to read them as "quotations." It is hard for most of us to remember that they were not "quotations" when they were uttered. They were vital, dynamic and fresh. They sprang from a heart and mind whose brilliance we cannot hope to match, but which we can at least strive to understand. Our best hope is to try to re-create the situation, the context, in which his words were spoken or the lesson taught. This, in turn, means that we must reconstruct the one-to-one or one-to-many basis for the original communication. He spoke to people, not to pews and pillars. And people responded with action and emotion.

The third problem most of us face when speaking Jesus' words is the fear of being theatrical. As we pointed out earlier, we are only theatrical or "arty" when our attention is on ourselves and our *performance.* If we stand apart from the reading and listen with awe to the beauty of our rolling tones, or turn our attention from what we are saying to perform some meticulously rehearsed gesture, our congregation will not believe what we are saying or that we are saying it to them. That is when we become "arty." There is little danger that we will overstep the bounds of decorum and good taste when our minds are attending to *what is being said* and our techniques are being used to support the demands of the material, with only the desire to share it with our listeners.

We will never know for sure whether the words we are given are exactly those which Jesus spoke, so we work with what we are given. As we have already noted, the words of Jesus are very similar if not identical in all four gospels, so it is safe to assume at least the spirit among the four versions and translations is accurate. And it is in the *spirit* of the gospels that many readers go astray. Careful analysis of the author's style and organization will help to guide our bodies and our voices.

To illustrate the point let's look at the parable of the sower (Lk 8:4–16; Matt 13:1–24; Mk 4:1–21). We must understand that Jesus told this parable to listeners who worked the land themselves and knew the way of seeds and growing things. His first sentence gets directly to what is relevant in their lives: "A sower went out to sow," an action they knew and understood well. It was applicable to their lives. As he goes on with the story, he uses the seed spread across the land to make his point about human and spiritual growth and how it affects the lives of people who listen and follow. The repeated reference to the seed, personalizing it with the word "others," keeps the audience's attention focused as the story progresses. Jesus concludes with the added words, "If you have ears to hear, then hear." Later, when his disciples come to him and ask an explanation of the parable, his tone and style change. He says:

> To you the secret of the kingdom of God has been given; but to those who are outside everything comes by way of parables, so that (as Scripture says) they may look and look, but see nothing; they may hear and hear but understand nothing; otherwise they might turn to God and be forgiven. . .You do not understand this parable? How then are you to understand any parable? (Mk 4:10–12).

He goes on to explain the references and the underlying meaning within the story. As you read the lesson aloud, let your ear pick up the nuances of language which mark Jesus' communication with the crowd and the different tone he adopts when speaking to those who form the inner circle of his fellowship.

There are many other examples of shifts in style which give us clear clues to the attitude we must adopt as we become this speaker in communication with his listeners. We become aware of how the occasion and the size and background of the audience influenced Jesus' communication style as well. And awareness of all these matters will allow us to use our voice and body skills most effectively to avoid becoming monotonous or boring. By using all we have learned we also discover the vitality of both the speakers and the speeches. These, in turn, help us to avoid a "liturgical" tone or any sense of vanity as we present these stories. They are important lessons, simple, and at the same time, deep in their meaning. Matthew writes that "a man's words flow out of what fills his heart" (12:34). This is certainly true of the people who fill the pages of the gospels. It behooves us then, as readers of these portions of scripture especially, to spend time studying the nature of each of the people we are presenting so that we can be sure of the heart and mind that controlled both the words and the actions.

The "Passion and Death" Passages

Most of the narrative units in the Christian scriptures are brief and simply organized. There is, however, one extended narrative that is vital, even pivotal, to a Christian reader. For most of us it is the climactic moment in Christian scripture. Significant to our purpose is the fact that this section is usually read in its entirety. And, though we are very familiar with it, having heard it for years, it is one of the most difficult sections in the Bible. It is, of course, the account of the passion and death of Jesus.

An initial problem arises in the way this climactic part of the gospels differs as it is told, first by one writer and then another. Matthew, Mark, and Luke make use of suspense. We are led on a lingering and sorrowful journey to the fulfillment of the ancient prophecies. When read so that the experience is truly shared, all three accounts are both moving and masterful. John, however, takes a somewhat different approach, one that needs real care in handling. Despite the differences, for modern listeners, John's account brings with it a relevance which is equal to the others in its ability to speak to an audience.

John puts the Last Discourse into a poetic style that fits the emotional intensity, giving both sweep and elevation to the content. John begins the eighteenth chapter with, "After these words." If we are beginning the lection here, it will be important to give a brief introduction to remind the congregation that Jesus and his disciples have just spent their last hours alone together, that the last supper has been shared, that Jesus is approaching the end of his mission on earth and that it is an end for which he alone knows the purpose. The actions that follow represent the culmination and realization of the words he has just spoken in the Upper Room.

The passion according to John is made up of five major units contained in chapters 18 and 19.[7] The units are both challenging and deceptively simple. They divide into a kind of play/filmscript form in which each unit is filled with both "stage directions" and the words of the speaker(s). Because it is written in this essentially dramatic form, the reading must not be rushed.

The first verse "sets the scene" in the garden of Gethsemane. John omits the prayer and agony included in the synoptic gospels and goes directly to the betrayal and arrest. The action begins with the appearance of the crowd. Then we are given the omniscient comment, "Knowing fully what was to happen to him, Jesus came out to them."[8] Then Jesus asks, "Whom are you looking for?" John then tells us that when Jesus identifies himself as the one they are looking for "they stepped back and fell to the ground." When Jesus asks his question a second time, their answer has none of the force or bravado of their first response. While they have been struck by the force of the presence they are confronting, they cannot change their plan. They can only repeat, "Jesus the Nazarene."

John digresses for a comment on how the event is a fulfillment of prophecy before he moves into the story of Peter's impetuous act, cutting off the ear of the high priest's servant. To add authenticity to his account, John adds a detail, the servant's name, which is not a part of any of the other gospel accounts. The episode is concluded in a single sentence telling us that Jesus was arrested, bound, and led away. The swiftness of this section seems astonishing in its compactness, despite the fact that the action is broken by what are, in fact, parenthetical explanations by the narrator.

The second major division is equally brief and crowded with action. It begins with the identification of Annas, his interrogation of Jesus, the slap on the face, Jesus' being sent to Caiaphas, and Peter's three denials. The problem for us here is that the two scenes—Annas' questioning of Jesus and Peter's denials—take place simultaneously, but in two separate locations. We must alternate descriptions of the scene taking place in the high priest's palace with those that are occurring in the courtyard of that building, shifting both focus and intensity from one to the other. It is no simple task for us to keep all these aspects unified and moving in the proper channels.

Our problems are further complicated by the fact that the scene in each setting has its own separate climax. Peter, with others, is warming himself by a charcoal fire. Although it is not made specific or clear, the assumption is that Peter is alone among strangers who are none too friendly. Further, there is a definite time progression to make clear. The climax of Peter's story is, in a way, a climax of the development of Peter's character. The climax is reached when Peter makes his third denial. But we are most moved, perhaps identifying with him, when the crowing of the cock, foretold only a few hours earlier, signals his failure to stand firmly for his Lord. The climax of the interrogation inside the palace is best seen as the blow on the cheek, in part at least because it is so unexpected.

The illegality of Jesus' trial has been discussed by scholars of Jewish law for years. If we remember Yahweh's words from Isaiah 45:19, "I

101

have said nothing in secret," they will help us keep Jesus' speeches from sounding arrogant to our congregations. He was replying with dignity and was well within his rights when he asked, "Why do you question me?" (18:21) Jewish law held that it was improper for an accused person to convict himself. The proper procedure would have been to question those who had heard him.

This is a difficult unit for us to handle. In large measure its effectiveness will depend on our abilities to keep both scenes and dialogue balanced, like a juggler keeping two objects in the air at the same time. We must concentrate on the characters in both scenes without losing sight of the pattern of the unit or of its place in the organization of the entire story[9].

The third unit (18:28 to 19:16) begins:

> Now, at daybreak, they took Jesus from Caiaphas to the praetorium.
> They did not enter the praetorium themselves for they had to avoid
> ritual impurity in order to eat the Passover supper. So Pilate came
> out to them.

The seven sections contained in this third unit alternate between the outside, where Pilate comes to meet Jesus and his captors, and the inside, where Pilate does his questioning. There is no problem of unity between the two settings here, because it is Pilate himself who takes us back and forth. John is very explicit with his connective devices, using such phrases as "Pilate went out again," " Once more Pilate went out," "Going back into the praetorium," and finally, "Then, at last, Pilate handed Jesus over to them to be crucified."

John's portrait of Pilate is brilliant. We are given a sharp, clear picture of a politician caught between two forces. On the one hand there is his logical Roman reason which finds no guilt in the accused by either Jewish or Roman law. This makes him reluctant to get involved in Jesus' death. The second force is public pressure and mob reaction from the very people Pilate is supposed to govern. In their first interview we sense Pilate's respect for and curiosity about his prisoner. He addresses Jesus as a man of equal intelligence and reason. There is also a touch of impatience as if this were one more problem to be coped with in a life full of confrontations and pressures. This problem differs from the others only in the obvious caliber of the accused man. Then there are the disturbing claims he is said to have made: the claim to kingship, which would infuriate Caesar and put Pilate's job in jeopardy, and the claim to being the Son of God.

Pilate's questions to Jesus are direct and seem to be worded to give him every chance to extricate himself from the situation. This would spare Pilate the necessity of solving the problem Jesus poses. Pilate points out that he, Pilate, is not a Jew and that it is Jesus' own countrymen who have brought him for judgment. And no one could ask for more straightforward and direct questions, requiring as they do simple, direct answers: "Are you the King of the Jews?" "What have you done?" "So, then, you are a king?" and finally "Truth? . . . And what is that?" This last question hints at a sophisticated cynicism that has grown out of Pilate's long political career. He is equally direct in his confrontation with the Jews. When he realizes they cannot be moved by persuasion, Pilate says finally, "I find no case against him."

The fourth unit in the drama moves swiftly to the climax, the crucifixion. In just two sentences John tell us that

> they took Jesus, and he went out, bearing his cross, to the place of a skull, which is called in Hebrew Golgotha. There they crucified him, and with him two others, one on either side, and Jesus between them.

Brief as these two sentences are, they are packed with *details* which must be described completely, given the full depth of implication which each segment contains. He was made to carry the instrument of his death to a place, the name of which was loaded with terrible connotations. Then, with no detail given, but agony implied, "they crucified him, and with him two others. . . ." Other people shared his agony that day, as many others had in the past and would share it in the future. We hear no more of these other two in John's account. He seems to use them more as symbols than as men. Next we hear the inscription, "Pilate also wrote the title and put it on the cross," and when the Jews objected, his words to them are direct and unequivocal, "What I have written, I have written."

John uses the time before Jesus' actual death to bring our attention down to the events transpiring around the cross. First he notes the soldiers "tossing"[10] for the seamless tunic; then he directs our attention to the small group of women. John shows Jesus' humanity, even at this time of great physical pain, as he expresses his concern for his mother and her future. But our attention is not to be distracted from the drama of the cross. John brings us back firmly, saying, "After this, aware that all was now finished, in order to bring the scripture to its complete fulfillment," he requests something to drink.

Jesus' last words are particularly telling in John's gospel. Matthew and Mark tell us he uttered a loud cry, but they give us no words. Luke has him address his last words directly to his heavenly Father. John gives us a simple statement that the long ministry and all the weights of the prophecies have now been accomplished. The words the Anchor translation of John gives are "he handed over his spirit." Other translations express it somewhat differently: "He said, 'It is finished'; and he bowed his head and gave up his spirit."[11]

The rest of the story flows quickly. Jesus' body is removed from the cross and buried quickly, bringing the narrative to a quiet, business-like close.

We must prepare carefully if we are to make this extended narrative come alive for our audiences. It is a difficult story to handle, but it is so central to the Christian faith, so moving and so relevant for today's world that, done with care, we find it contains an added level of identity for us today. If we in any way nullify or fail to utilize all the dramatic, "story" narrative qualities in this account, whether it be John's or from the synoptic gospels, we obstruct the complete communication required of the story. And any such personal obstruction, any overdrawing on our part, is the height of egocentricity. God gave us responsive minds, voices, bodies. He expects us to use them fully when we proclaim his message.

The Acts of the Apostles

The Acts of the Apostles, which completes the narratives of the Christian scripture, is an episodic series of accounts of the early church and its leaders. The writing is generally conceded to come from the writer of Luke's gospel, since there appear to be links between the final passages of that gospel and the beginning chapter of Acts. The book has been described as, in part, a statement of the problems of the followers/believers in Jesus as the Christ, in the Gentile world they were charged to serve.[12] The major problem relates to the statement made earlier regarding the Jewish Christians. They made up the bulk of the membership of the church during its first century. Their question was: How could Gentiles become Christians unless they embraced the covenant of Judaism? Those first Christians had done so; the new converts, perhaps, should be required to do the same. The dilemma becomes the basis for the episodes which Luke recounts in the book. It has been suggested that one theme of the Acts is one of trying to understand the character of the church that was emerging in the Roman world of the first century. This narrative, tied so closely to the conclusion of Luke's own gospel, suggests that the stories relate to some of our contemporary faith discussions.

Each chapter has its own set of characters and its own organization. When dealt with as individual story/dramas, the book does not present any unusual problems for us as worship leaders. The unifying principle throughout is the recounting of the progress of the mission assumed by the apostles.[13] Luke mixes style much more freely in Acts than in his gospel, so we need to pay attention to both style and organization, since these are basic clues to the best reading of these sections. Study of this sort will yield a great deal in the way of variety in our reading presentations.

Notes

1. Richard Longenecker observes that the term *Jewish Christians* "indicates early Christians whose conceptual frame of reference and whose expressions were rooted in Semitic thought generally and Judaism in particular." Perhaps because of the Judaic storytelling tradition for the gospels much of what we said about the Hebrew scripture in the preceding chapter is equally applicable here. Both the Hebrew and Christian scriptures exhibit the presence of intuitive minds with the capacity for wonder and for immediate response to the messages of the prophet-messiah. Both are characterized by concrete thinking and strong emotional undercurrents. William Stegner points out, however that, for today's readers the problem of understanding Christian scripture is compounded by the fact that "Not only [are] the narrative[s] nearly two thousand years old, but [they] were formulated by an oriental people whose mindset was quite different from that of the Greeks and Romans, our intellectual ancestors."

Richard Longenecker, *The Christology of Early Jewish Christianity, Studies in Biblical Theology*, 2nd. ed. ser. 17 (London: SCM, 1970), p. 3.

2. *The Gospel of Thomas*, translated from a Coptic text, has become one of

the recent additions to our understanding of the gospels. While the first fragments of the book were discovered in 1897, the fully translated text did not appear until 1945. It is currently available in paperback, published in 1992 by HarperCollins Publishers, New York. There were several other gospels which predated the four which appear today in our Bibles. The choice of these four was made by the Council of Nicea. The earlier books may be found in the New Testament Apocrypha.

3. As Roderick A. F. MacKenzie, S.J., points out in his *New Testament Reading Guide*:

. . .the authors of these books were writing for a particular public, their contemporary fellow-Christians; their immediate purpose was the "edification," i.e., the building-up, of the church of their own day. Though they may vaguely have foreseen that their work would be treasured for future generations, still they had primarily in view the contemporary situation, and their teaching represents their own particular stage in the understanding and development of "the Good News of Jesus Christ." Further, the gospel writers were speaking to both Jews and Gentiles in Rome and in Greece as well as to the people of Palestine.

New Testament Reading Guide (Collegeville, MN: The Liturgical Press, 1964).

4. One of the observations made by the redaction critics is that these speeches are almost identically worded in all four writings. This is seen as yet another proof of a common, root text from which all four were drawn and unanimous authorial unwillingness to presume to change what was traditionally attributed to Jesus.

5. A unique point of difference between the synoptic gospels and John's account is that in John's record of the event a boy in the crowd has five barley loaves and two fishes whereas in the other accounts it is assumed that the provisions had been brought by the apostles. Despite these differences, the other facts are precisely the same in all four gospels, including the number of loaves and fishes, the number that were fed, and the amount which was gathered up after they all had eaten as much as they wanted. And the dialogue is essentially the same.

6. God the father speaks directly and in his own person far less frequently in the Christian scripture than in the Hebrew, but we would do the account of the Jesus' transfiguration great injustice if we failed to express the pride and love we hear as God speaks to and of his Son as "the Chosen One" and "the Beloved."

7. Chapter 17 might well be included in this section since, as a pastor friend, Larry Hard, has suggested, Chapter 17 is what might best be called "The Other or Extended Lord's Prayer."

8. Text for this section is drawn from The Anchor Bible, vol.29a.

9. It should be noted that John does not give us a report of Jesus' question-

ing by Caiaphas nor does he tell us about the meeting of the Sanhedrin, a scene which the other gospels include. In omitting these two confrontations John loses some of the suspense produced by the others but the loss is compensated through speed in keeping the events moving to the inevitable climax and through sharper focus on the characters within the tragedy.

10. Other versions use the words "cast lots." As John points out, these words have their roots in Hebrew scripture, specifically in Psalms 22:18.

11 These words seem to have originated in the King James Version and have been preserved in various translations down to the *New Revised Standard Version*, published by Thomas Nelson in 1989.

12. Neil M. Flanagan, O.S.M., *New Testament Reading Guide: The Acts of the Apostles* (Collegeville, MN: The Liturgical Press, 1964), pp. 6–7.

13. Questions arise about the authenticity of Acts as an historical document. Some commentators prefer to see the book as a kind of apologia. While it traces the development of the new religion it also is aimed at convincing the Roman authorities that the new Christians were not hostile to their laws and therefore not be persecuted as a threat to their society. The book also reveals how the teaching of the new faith in Christ became more precise, although there continues to be discussion about the date(s) and place of the writing.

8

The Epistles

Preparing and reading the epistles should be the easiest job we, as liturgists, have. After all, they were letters of instruction *meant to be read aloud* to congregations of Christian believers. A reading from the epistles is part of every Sunday's lection. But, when we listen to these letters read, we become aware that the task is larger than it looks. What are the problems? Why are they so difficult?

For one thing, the complexities of the content and the allusions to events beyond our immediate knowledge become barriers both to our understanding, and to our intelligent presentation, of this material. Some of the difficulty begins with the fact that the epistles are an entirely different kind of literature than we have been dealing with in the other parts of the Bible. It is important for us to be aware of the *differences* between a selection which is built around a time-bound description, those stories whose unity is essentially *narrative* in structure, and the epistolary style of the *letters*.

The epistles have raised some thorny issues among scholars as well. The main questions regard the matter of authorship. You may have read some of the research which questions who the real authors of some of the epistles were. We have chosen not to enter these debates. Rather, to simplify our task and more practically serve our needs, we shall assume that the letters credited to Paul were written or dictated by him and those credited to John were written by him, and so forth. We do not believe that this assumption represents slipshod scholarship on our part.[1] We are concerned with our roles as lector/worship leaders not as textual research scholars. We have said before that we must make use of all that textual scholars have discovered, but some of the scholarship seems to define minutiae that do not assist our congregations in discovering the message a lection contains. Nor are we especially concerned with re-creating the physical characteristics of the writer himself.[2] We are the medium, the transmitters of the *message*. Our concern is with the literature that has been produced.

Then why are the epistles difficult to read? What is the difference whether the material is narrative in form or in the form of letters?

A narrative may teach a lesson by telling us what happened to someone on a certain day and at a certain moment. Letters, on the other hand, are usually responses to situations and events. They are not confined to a *specific* moment. As we know from our own experience, letters, and in this case the writings we call the epistles[3], rely on different types of word choice and sentence construction to achieve their purpose. And one of our tasks is to understand those objectives.[4]

In our own case when we write a letter, the choices we make in words or constructions are often dictated both by the intended recipient and by the reason for the letter. We may write to advise a friend about a problem we or they are having. We may want to share news or express a sentiment. And, just as in our own letters, the choices made by the writer(s) here are usually defined by that writer's relation to the addressee(s). He may be trying to clarify a theological point, to instruct or, perhaps, to correct a way of life as he perceives it to be lived by members of one of the congregations. The epistles are always messages directed to specific audiences. They were written or dictated to convey some relevant information. As liturgists, then, our principal concern begins with both the mindset of the writer, as we learn it through an examination of his writing, and the life-styles and attitudes of the intended receivers whom he is addressing.

A second concern relates to the reason for the letter. Sometimes the intention of the letter is to be persuasive, especially to those people of the world who have not yet become convinced of the joy of the good news of the gospel. It appears that Paul's letter to the church at Rome and the letter designated as "to the Ephesians" may have been circulated beyond Rome to Paul's Asian churches for this exact purpose.[5] Each epistle assumes its own style, a style which we must adopt as our own when we are reading for our congregations. Discovery of authorial technique, intended audience, and purpose need to be part of our preparation to read the letter aloud.

We would like to offer a word of advice. There are many very good commentaries on the market—and probably on your pastor's shelf.

Reading one with regard to the assigned lection will help to focus and aid in the discovery of audience and the purpose for the lection you are preparing to read. You can find commentaries in libraries—probably your own church's library—as well as in bookstores. They are definitely worth the investment of your time as you prepare the lection passages.

Let's take a moment to distinguish between the private and the public letters in the Bible. Those written by Paul to Timothy tend to fall into the "private" category. They are a kind of pastoral instruction. They may have been open letters, addressed to Timothy, but intended to be shared with others. But, as we will see, the tone of these letters is informal and affectionate. And the organization of the body of the letter is dictated, in part, by the close relationship Paul felt with the younger man. The bulk of the epistles, however, were intended for public reading. They were sent to the leaders of a group to be shared with the faithful, probably in a meeting of the entire company. They are instructional, doctrinal, mainly persuasive and rhetorical both in style and content. In many ways they are close to speeches or orations both in their method of organization and in their adaptability to a large audience. It is this oratorical nature which should make them more comfortable for us to handle.

In terms of form, Paul followed the pattern of organization used for personal letters of his day. Each begins with a greeting, which is followed by a prayer. The prayer is followed by words of thanksgiving. The body, the main purpose of the letter, makes up the major portion of the communication. And the whole is concluded with special notes and personal greetings. We find this pattern repeated in most of Paul's letters.[6]

Corinthians

Let's begin our examination of Paul's letters with his first epistle to the church at Corinth. This is one of Paul's "public" letters, meant to be shared with all the faithful in Corinth. It serves well as a beginning point, because most of us have heard some or all of this letter for many years. It will also give us some clues to his word choices and the ways in which his letters are constructed. We may never have thought of 1 Corinthians in terms of literary *style*, simply because it is so familiar. And, perhaps because of this familiarity, when it is read aloud as part of a service, the first letter to the church at Corinth stands in great need of being revitalized. Earlier in this book we looked briefly at Corinthians in terms of the general principles of its construction and unity. At that time we observed Paul's use of first- and second-person pronouns, "we," "you," and "I." We commented on his opening and closing statements to the Corinthians as he expresses his affection and concern for them as followers of Jesus. We looked briefly at the grouping of ideas and the transitions from one to another.

But, as we read the first letter to the Corinthians more closely we get the feeling that Paul must have begun with a fully planned outline for the letter in mind (and, perhaps, in hand) before he started. He certainly seems to have had the letters he was answering in mind. He begins by expressing affection for the membership of the church at Corinth:

> I continually thank my God for you because of the favor he has bestowed on you in Christ Jesus, in whom you have been richly endowed with every gift of speech and knowledge. Likewise, the witness I bore to Christ has been so confirmed among you that you lack no spiritual gift as you wait for the revelation of our Lord Jesus Christ (1 Cor 1:4–7 NAB).

In this first letter to that church the list of faults within the membership must have been personally affective to Paul. He had converted these people. Yet he always returns to their privileged position in the structure of the new church and their knowledge of truth. He continues to imply that he is confident about their personal and moral strength. Almost without exception, the various units of the letter end with an expression of his own sense of harmony with and affection for them, the feeling with which he began the epistle.

Paul's method of transition from one major unit of thought to another is usually very direct. At times he seems to be saying, "Now, the next thing on my list . . . ," but the ideas are grouped in such a way that they fall into related categories. He begins the body of the letter with a discussion of the need for unity in the church, and he returns to a renewed call for that need for unity at the end: "You are not your own; you were bought with a price. So glorify God in your body" (6:19–20).

Paul then starts down the list of reported transgressions. He speaks of incest, which he says he considers even worse than the practices of the pagans.[7] This leads to talk about the pagan courts. And "pagan practices" lead to condemnation of the worst sin of the pagan community: the practice of fornication. He moves from that vice to a discussion of marriage and virginity.

His comments on food offered to the idols in the city, with which he begins chapter 8, seems to form a break in the flow of the letter. But the reference to food for pagan gods depends on its connection to the pagan customs he discussed a moment earlier. Paul then compares pagan practices to the righteousness of Christian wisdom and conduct. Pagan gifts are contrasted with spiritual gifts. And "spiritual gifts" begin his discussion of Christian love. He develops the claims of love and the control love places upon freedom.

But, by the end of chapter 10, he returns, again, to talk about pagan practices and "demons," which leads to a discussion of decorum in public worship, "Be imitators of me, as I am of Christ" (11:1). After chiding them again about divisiveness, he scolds them about the report he has had of indecorous behavior on the part of some members when they come together as a church. He calls for the restraint which is the mark of the worship of Jesus when his supper is celebrated, then he returns to the view of spiritual gifts with which he began chapter 12.

There then follows what must be ranked among the best-known of all the passages to be found in either scripture: the justly famous and beautifully constructed unit on the importance of love as the greatest of all the gifts we will ever receive (chap. 13). He moves smoothly to love as the gift of prophecy and the practice of "speaking in tongues" (14:6), and then adds a final word on the ordering of services of worship and of the regulation of all spiritual gifts, saying that "all things should be done decently and in order."

Chapter 15, which concerns itself with the question of life after death, opens with citations of Jesus' death, burial, and resurrection. Paul recalls all of the people to whom the risen Christ appeared, concluding with his own encounter on the Damascus road. The chapter ends with a hymn of triumph.

After a few words about financial support, Paul concludes the letter by returning to the opening tone of affection for those special people he will soon be visiting. He recommends Timothy to them as "doing the Lord's work." He finally asks their charity for the Stephanas family who "have worked hard to help the saints." And the letter ends as it began, with declarations of his special love for the receivers—those he has often referred to as "brothers' and "dearest children."

Throughout the letter, Paul follows the theme that the church at Corinth has been blessed with every form of spiritual (and material) gift. He continues to contrast their gifts with the ways of "pagans," alternating the two life-styles. But with these gifts come the need for unity within the congregation and fidelity to God.

As lectors, it is important that we keep these basic themes in mind as we read any portion of this letter, since they unify the entire structure.

As we prepare any lection from the epistles, we need to be aware of both the words and the *music* as the language is arranged in the letter. We will return to the "music" of Corinthians in a moment; the words are our concern now.

The second letter to the Corinthians suffers by comparison to the first in that it is less well organized. Some scholars believe it contains fragments from an earlier lost letter. Despite its lack of clear organization, it contains much of the unique style of which Paul was a master. The section which begins with chapter 1, verse 12 continues in the high style of which Paul was capable all the way through chapter 6, verse 10. Throughout this section Paul's use of oratorical devices is nothing short of brilliant. His use of rhetorical questions, beginning with 1:17 is an early example: "Was I vacillating when I wanted to [come back to you]? Do I make my plans according to ordinary human standards . . . ?" Paul leads from questions such as these about his own actions to the sure and positive answer in life, the risen Christ. Look for a moment at the structure of this verse (we have rearranged it to make a point):

The Son of God,
Christ Jesus,
proclaimed among you by us
(by Silvanus and Timothy, I mean,
   as well as myself),
was never a blend of Yes and No.
With him it was,
and is,
Yes. (2 Cor. 1:19 NEB)

The style is almost poetic in the way in which Paul pursues his point down to the single word "Yes."[8] This epistle also employs some unique sensate imagery which occurs rarely in these letters. Near the end of the second chapter, he writes:

> But thanks be to God, who in Christ always leads us in triumph, and through us spreads the fragrance of the knowledge of him everywhere. For we are the aroma of Christ to God among those who are being saved and among those who are perishing, to one a fragrance from death to death, to the other a fragrance from life to life (2 Cor. 2:15–16)

There is no such example in his first letter to Corinth.

In chapter 6, verse 11, Paul switches to a warm, intimate tone with "Men of Corinth, we have spoken very frankly to you; we have opened our heart wide to you all. . . . In fair exchange then (may a father speak so to his children?) open wide your hearts to us." He reminds them that they are the true temples of God; he expresses joy at their repentance. He then begins a "stewardship campaign," soliciting funds for the church at Jerusalem. He continues the letter with a strong and forceful statement of his faith. He warns them to be on guard against false apostles, restating his own suffering as an apostle. He ends the letter, as he has the first, with a blessing—one which has become a benediction in many modern churches through its strength and its simplicity.

Galatians and Romans

These two letters deal with essentially the same problem: the relation between Judaism and Christianity. But there are some very sharp differences between them. While Romans is written to prepare the congregation for his visit, a visit to a church he had never seen but one whose support he needed as he began planning his evangelizing in the lands to the west, his communication to the church at Galatia appears to be Paul's reaction to a situation that existed there.

Let's begin with Galatians. Paul is responding to the Galatian view that an individual must become a Jew first before becoming a Christian. And he is countering their question of his authority, his apostolic claim, since he was not, in fact, one of the twelve who journeyed for three years with Jesus. He talks about the beginnings of the church and about his own life. But the principal thrust of the letter has to do with the issue of Judaism and the law. We mentioned that the first converts to the new religion were Jews. We used the term "Jewish Christians" there. But Paul's ministry was to the Gentile world. He was not conversant with the church in Jerusalem until some time after he had started his campaign of evangelization. But, in many cities where congregations had begun, the first members were Jewish Christians. And in the area of Galatia, especially, these Jewish Christians were insisting that Gentile ("Greek") converts should become Jews first, and adhere to Mosaic law, before becoming followers of the Christ. This letter to the church in Galatia rebuts that view very forcefully. In fact, some commentators go so far as to say that Christianity would have remained a branch, a cult of Judaism, if Paul had not written as he did. The commentator who has written the headnote to this letter in The New Oxford Annotated Bible says: "The declaration of principles reiterated in these six chapters made Christianity a world religion instead of a Jewish sect."[9]

In the Galatian letter, Paul addresses the issue of conversion to Christianity through redemption. Judaism taught that salvation came as a reward for good works; that a person could *earn* his way to Heaven through adherence to the *law*. Paul argues that adherence to the law was not always the standard. To prove his point, Paul offers the example of Abraham. Considered the patriarch/father of the faith, Abraham, says Paul, could not have lived under the code of law, since Moses did not proclaim that law until four hundred and thirty years *after* Abraham lived. Paul's point is that God shows his love to us through his grace, that transcends works: "for if justification comes through the law, then Christ died for nothing" (2:31).

Paul's last words in this letter speak simply and directly to the matter of grace: "May the grace of our Lord Jesus Christ be with your spirit, brothers and sister. Amen." This simpler, less personal form of the letter has led to the conclusion pointed out earlier: that this was a "general" letter, to be shared by all the churches in Asia Minor. No matter the reason, the letter to the Galatians is one of the most powerful statements of Christian doctrine we have today.

When we turn to the Letter to the Romans, we find a very different style of writing. For one thing, Paul was writing to a church he really didn't know. He had no part in the formation of the church, no personal contact at all. As some commentators have written, Romans is the closest of all the letters to being a theological treatise. It details Paul's position with regard to the gospel in a way that has been called his "theological last will and testament."[10] It is the longest of the epistles, and, in consequence, is considered to be the most influential. As with Galatians, Paul is once again showing that salvation is available to Jew and Gentile alike. He traces God's plan from Adam to Christ. Reconciliation and forgiveness are meshed with justification. The whole letter carries a tone of authority and dignity—a style matching Paul's less-than-personal acquaintance with the members of the church at Rome. In every sense, it is a "teaching" letter.

By contrast, the two letters to Timothy and the letter to Titus are certainly more friendly, more intimate, and more private than those found in Paul's public writing. From the opening salutations, we are aware of an entirely different relation between the writer and the recipient than we found in Corinthians or Galatians. These private letters are less extended and much warmer in tone. Both letters to Timothy begin: "Paul, an apostle of Christ Jesus . . . To Timothy, my . . . child: Grace, mercy, and peace from God the father and Christ Jesus our Lord." There is no comment on faith, doctrine, or behavior. The blessing is direct and simple. In similar manner, the greeting to Titus also uses the "From . . . To . . ." format, but between them Paul drops in a mini-sermon and a statement of his position and mission.

The conclusions of the public and private letters also show real differences in relationship between the writer and the receivers. Paul uses eight short sentences to conclude Corinthians. The greetings, wishes, and love he expresses are those of a Christian leader for a group of Christians rather than of one person to another.

Even when only a small part of a letter is being read, it is important to try to re-create the tone and the degree of intimacy shown in the opening and closing sections. These will serve as guides to the relationship between the writer and the receiver. And attention to the tone of the letter will help us understand the persuasive appeals used throughout the writing.

A brief look at the word choices in these four letters reveals a consistency and harmony between the openings and closings. In 1

Corinthians, the words carry the tone of a leader and teacher: words like "witnesses," "I appeal," "preach," "salvation," "knowledge," "foolishness," "servants." These are the words of an authority figure, spoken with confidence and strength, tempered with affection.

The word choices in the letters to Timothy form a striking contrast to Corinthians. Here the words have the tone of friendship: "As I asked you," "I ask you to remember," "You are well aware," "Do your best to come," and the words listing the qualities of a church leader: "temperate," "discreet," "kind," "peaceable." Chapter 3 contains numerous words of courage: "confidence," "good soldier," "dedicated," "duty," "brave," "power," all of which reflect the strength of the writer, despite his imprisonment and reflect as well his certainty of Timothy's equal strength.

In the letter to Titus the word choices are even simpler, indicating a willingness to explain and clarify: "You see," "The reason," "I want you to be," "remember," "behavior." While paralleling the advice given to Timothy, the diction is much simpler, a fact which may reflect his attitude toward Titus, whom he knew well. What is more likely is that Paul adjusted his vocabulary to fit the group with whom Titus would probably share the letter. The reason behind the simplicity is of less importance to us than the fact that Paul used these words and shorter, more direct sentences to impart his ideas.

The Rhythms of Prose

A few pages back we made mention of the idea that our task as lector/worship leader includes both the words of a selection and its music. What is the *music* of *prose*? You are already aware that poetry produces a kind of music both through word choices and the variety of rhythms—rising or falling, quick and light or ponderous—the words produce. These rhythms are dependent upon the writer's arrangement of words, using their stressed/accented or unstressed/unaccented syllables. The poetry analysts have given names to the various measures, or "meters," of poetry, depending on how syllables are distributed in the pattern of words within a line. The names themselves go back to the poets of early Greece, hence: "iambic" or "trochaic," all the way through six more descriptors. We have become so used to the rhythms of poetry that we have come to ignore the "rising" and "falling" rhythms, insistent or languid rhythms in prose. Yet a rhythm is produced in a prose line, too, depending on how and where the accented and unaccented syllables fall.

Describing prose rhythms is not nearly so vital as being aware that they *exist*, but *finding* stressed syllables, and *marking* them, IS important. Doing this detective work provides you, and your listeners, with a clear map to the way thoughts and ideas that are being expressed by the writer. For example, look at these lines from 1 Corinthians:

> Isn't that obvious from all the jealousy and wrangling that there is among you, from the way you go on behaving like ordinary people? What could be more unspiritual than your slogans, "I am for Paul" and "I am for Appolos?"

Now, take a pencil and mark the accented or stressed syllables within the key words in the passage. (You may prefer to write the lines out on another piece of paper to do this.)

Look back at the markings. How did you decide which ones stood out and which ones didn't?

You probably began with marking nouns, then verbs. They tell us *who* did *what.* You may also have noticed that words with more than one syllable—polysyllabic words—had one syllable that was pushed or accented more than the others, words like "SHEP-herd," "be-SIDE," "WATers," or, as in words we just used, "SYLL-a-ble" and "AC-cent-ed."

You then may have moved on to adjectives, which add color to the person or place and continued to adverbs, describing how an action was carried out or how a person felt.

You probably also noticed that you did NOT mark those parts of speech called articles—"the" or "a," pronouns, like "he," "you,"or "them," or conjunctions, "and," "but," "or." In fact, if you went back and read it aloud, you found that you *automatically* stressed certain syllables because that was the way the passage made sense.

We have done some marking on the same passage. See how we compare. Stressed words/syllables are capitalized and separated with /marks.

> IS/n't that OB/vi/ous from ALL the JEAL/ou/sy and WRANG/ling that there IS a/MONG you, from the WAY you go ON be/HA/ving like OR/di/na/ry PE/ople? WHAT could be

MORE UN/SPIR/it/u/al than your SLO/gans, "I am for PAUL and "I am for Ap/POL/los?"

If we were to go through and complete the lines, marking both stressed/accented and unaccented/unstressed syllables, you would be able to see, as well as hear, the way in which Paul's lines set up a musical rhythm which matches the content: /xx x /xx x / x /xx x /x x x / x/ x. Look at, and listen to, the insistent, demanding, almost table-pounding rhythm of

COME to your SENS/es,(/ x x /x)
be/HAVE PRO/per/ly, (x/ /xx)
and leave SIN a/LONE. (x x / x/) (1 Cor 15:34).

It will take a little time to get used to marking, and listening to, prose rhythms, but, once you get the idea into your head, your readings will *sing* as well as *speak* to the hearts of your congregation.

Helping Today's Audiences Understand

We have examined each of these letters closely, with the help of commentaries and pastoral friends, we have determined what prompted the letter, who the recipients were, and the circumstances of the writing. But we may still be troubled about how to involve our congregations with the problem(s) addressed in the portion which has been selected for the morning's lection. Where do we begin?

We begin by identifying, as closely as possible, with the *writer*. We need to try to think as he was thinking when he dictated or wrote in these circumstances. How did Paul or John feel about the people they were contacting when they were composing the letter? For Paul, the answer often is that he felt very responsible for the churches he was writing to. He had converted many of these people; he had helped in the creation of many of their churches. He was trying to help these new Christians begin a new life-style. He writes as both a teacher/interpreter of the gospel and as a fellow struggler with the distractions and temptations he finds in his own world. And he has a great sense of *energy* and *dedication*. So our first task is to believe the truth of what is being conveyed, entering into the discussion as vigorously as Paul

119

himself would do if he were standing with us at the lectern. It is Paul's letter, and we must use as much of "Paul," his mind and his energy, as we can find.

When Paul was writing, he had as clear a picture of his audience as we have of ours. And his thoughts went to people he knew in those places. His ideas and arguments are still sound, and human beings haven't changed as much as we might wish they had over the centuries. So, our task is to see Paul's people in our sanctuary. We speak in Paul's words, using the attitudes we have discovered in his writing, to a group of interested people. And our congregations are just as interested in finding help for their lives today as were the early Christians of Paul's time. But vitality and interest on our part is a major factor. Generations of bad, or at least indifferent, readings of this material must be compensated for.

With the type of material we find in the epistles, *eye contact* becomes a matter of some importance. This means familiarity and rehearsal sufficient for us to get off the page and out to the people. Most of Paul's writings are quite challenging and direct. We need to use every bit of our energy—voice and body—to make the words come alive.

Notes

1. We believe it truly does not matter whether Paul actually wrote all the letters credited to him, or if John, whose letters bear his name was not really named John or if he was not the same John who wrote the gospel. Those facts are irrelevant to our task as liturgists. We are concerned only with what is on the printed page. We will simply accept that someone named something wrote the messages we find, and that the letters are authentic for their time and place.

2. A contemporary practice adopted by some presenters of the epistles includes costuming, insofar as the person can, in the dress of the time. It is our opinion that this practice oversteps the bounds of our task. A congregation is far more apt to consider the costume rather than the content of the message being presented for their thoughtful consideration.

3. The term "epistle" is a bit misleading here. The dictionary definition of an epistle refers to a writing done in formal tone and elevated style. William Barclay suggests that many of Paul's letters were written in moments when Paul was, in Barclay's words, "pouring out a torrent of words, while his secretary raced to get them down," as he responds to a group or a situation.

William Barclay, *The Letter to the Romans* (Philadelphia, Pa.: The Westminster Press, 1955), p. xix.

4. Barclay points out a major problem we face with the epistles. He likens the reading of these letters from the Bible to listening to just one-half of a telephone conversation; we never know what the other half of the conversation is. In truth, we are never completely sure of what motivated the writer in the first place.

c.f. *The Letter to the Romans*, p. xv.

5. Barclay points out that the same is true of the letter to the Ephesians. He refers to Ephesians as a "circular letter," one passed from one community to the next. Barclay indicates that there is none of the usual personal greeting or salutations in the letter, despite the fact that Paul spent some time in Ephesus. Barclay offers a rather lengthy explanation of both this letter and the "circular letter" in general. See his Letter to the Ephesians, in *The Letters to the Galatians and the Ephesians* (Edinburgh: St. Andrews Press, 1960), p.73–ff.

6. Barclay describes the structure of private letters of Paul's day, showing this pattern and documenting it from the epistles, in "The Ancient Letters" section of his introduction to *The Letter to the Romans* (Philadelphia: Westminster Press, 1957), p. xvii.

7. Historians tell us that Corinth, as a major seaport of its day, was rampant with all manner of pagan practices. The number of prostitutes was quite large, again, because of the number of transient sailors who came through the port. There were any number of temples to the gods of other cultures. In all, Paul's flock in Corinth was living in a society that was about as un-Christian as any in the world.

8. This passage from *The New English Bible*, p. N.T. 227. Typography has been rearranged to illustrate style.

9. Preface to "The Letter of Paul to the Galatians," in *The New Oxford Annotated Bible*, ed. Bruce R. Metzger and Roland E. Murphy (New York: Oxford University Press, 1991), p. 263 NT.

10 Barclay, *The Letter to the Romans* (Philadelphia: Westminster Press, 1960) p. xxi.

9

Revelation and Apocryphal Literature

Blessed is the one who reads aloud the words of prophecy, and blessed are those who hear and who keep what is written in it; for the time is near Revelation 1:3 (NRSV).

On most Sundays of the church year, our lections call for readings from the prophets of Israel. Isaiah, Jeremiah, Micah, Amos, Hosea, or Ezekiel are some of the more frequently used sources. Much less frequently the lections contain passages from the book of Revelation. But in both of these sources, the prophets of the Hebrew scriptures and the writer, or writers, of Revelation have described their visions of God's plan for his world.

The Nature of Prophecy

It does seem fitting that we should be discussing the oral reading of these prophetic revelations immediately following the epistles, since the two share a great deal. For one thing, like Paul and the author(s) of Revelation, the major prophets of the Hebrew scripture usually speak in their own voices. And all of these spokespersons—the older prophets bringing the words of Yahweh, Paul and the writer(s) of Revelation speaking for Christ—reveal God's new world order for his people.

This idea of a new world order takes several forms. From the earliest prophets, it is usually called "Historical eschatology." Eschaton means "endtimes" and looks forward to what God will do in the future to accomplish the words of the prophet. However, nearly every prophet expected that God would act within the foreseeable future, that is, within the ordinary historical developments that were unfolding. Later books such as Daniel and the book of Revelation in the Christian scripture have a more extreme viewpoint. These books show a passionate conviction that God will overthrow the present world and remake it or restore it so that good will triumph and the wicked perish. The name given to such material is *apocalyptic*.

Today, the word is apt to conjure up pictures of destruction, devastation and war—some variation on the end of the world we know—the sort of view which moviegoing patrons got in the film *Apocalypse Now*. The dictionary, however, offers a more positive view. One dictionary defines the word "apocalyptic" as:

> One of the Jewish and Christian writings of 200 B.C. to 150 A.D. marked by pseudonymity [i.e., bearing a fictitious name for the author], symbolic imagery, and the expectation of an imminent cataclysm in which God destroys the ruling powers of evil and *raises the righteous to life* in a messianic kingdom . . . 2. *something viewed as a prophetic revelation*.[1]

The prophets and the writer of Revelation share a common basis for their pronouncements: The new order builds on the tradition of the past. The Christian scriptures draw on Hebrew sources to validate Jesus' role as the Son of God. As we hear every year, the prophecies of Isaiah are a regular part of our Advent readings. And many of his words, as well as others found in Revelation, speak to us in the music of the season as they were incorporated into George Frederick Handel's magnificent *Messiah*. Isaiah's pronouncements, along with others of the time, are used to show that Jesus' birth had been foretold in Jewish literature for centuries—that the miracle of Jesus' birth was a fulfillment of *prophecy*. So these visionary sections of the two scriptures come down to us, both as guides and as inspirations to a new life promised by God for our world.

Another similarity between the prophecies and the epistles, important to us in our work as worship leaders, is that both the prophets and the authors of the epistles were writing for a particular *segment* of the population—a particular audience. In both scriptures, the messages were designed to *keep* the faithful loyal to the religions they espoused. The prophets' aim was to preserve Israel's devotion to

Yahweh; the writers of the epistles wrote to encourage new converts to stay on the path of salvation offered by Jesus. But, the messages of the prophecies and the epistles are worded in very different ways. Paul's letters are often built on the legalistic framework of Judaic law, with which he was very conversant. They deal almost exclusively with the *logic* and the mystery of *grace* offered by the new Christian faith. In contrast to this style, the prophets, both in the Hebrew scriptures and in the book of Revelation, use highly graphic, highly colorful descriptions of the visions they are recounting. The prophets use their depictions to detail the severe consequences which will follow if the Israelites transgress the law of Yahweh. The writers of Revelation describe some of the same alternatives for the followers of Christ who fall away from God's grace. In each case, the pictures are verbally colorful, filled with the sights and sounds of those visions. And both— prophecies and Revelation—were very clear in their depiction of the situations that existed at the time of the writing. We will discuss the differences—as well as the similarities—between the prophecies and Revelation shortly, but let's begin with the prophets.

At about the middle of the eighth century B.C. the long tradition of prophecy underwent a major change. The whole craft had fallen into disrepute, largely because of the numbers of charlatans who had used the tradition for their own use. But with the advent of Amos and Hosea in the north, and Isaiah and Micah in the south, the period known as "classic prophecy" began. The words of these four, and those whose voices followed, have found an important place in our Bibles in the books that bear their names.

Many annotated Bibles and commentaries cite approximate dates for the major prophets and, while there is often disagreement about these dates, there is general agreement that, more than any other biblical writings, the books of prophecy have been edited, emended, condensed or expanded by many writers over the centuries. The result is often an uneven, changing sense of the speaker from one section of a book to another. It does seem clear that all of the early prophecies were delivered orally and written down much later, either from memory or from notes gathered for the purpose. Thus, when we speak of *writings* we are not using the term in any modern sense. Our concern will be with the general properties of prophetic "writing" as those qualities affect our task of communicating prophetic visions to modern-day audiences. Again, we will be making use of our skills as narrators, but we will also be developing new skills in handling the poetic language, the expressions used by the prophets to explain their visions.

The Power of Prophetic Speech

The proclamations of the prophets in Hebrew scriptures were drawn from the depths of their beings. They spoke as men who had been called to a divine and difficult vocation. Several of them tell us of their calling, and, often, of their reluctance to accept that call as well. Jonah even tries to run away from the summons. One of the well-known voices, Ezekiel, details his call from God by telling date, place and circumstance:

> In the thirtieth year, in the fourth month, on the fifth day of the month, as I was among the exiles by the river Chebar, the heavens were opened, and I saw visions of God. On the fifth day of the month, (it was the fifth year of the exile of King Jehoiachin), the word of the Lord came to Ezekiel, the priest, the son of Buzi, in the land of the Chaldeans by the river Chebar; and the hand of the Lord was upon him there (Ezekiel 1:1-3, RSV).

As you heard, the text suggests a second writer, filling in details left out by the first. But the attempt to validate the prophet's claim to speak from his vision of God is certainly well stated. Ezekiel's prophecies are perhaps best remembered for his images of the "wheels-within-wheels" which accompanied the creatures flying above him in the vision.

Certainly one of the most vivid and beautiful accounts of the calling of a prophet is Isaiah's description of his own summons to service:

> In the year that King Uzziah died I saw the Lord sitting upon a throne, high and lifted up; and his train filled the temple. Above him stood the seraphim; each had six wings: with two he covered his face, and with two he covered his feet, and with two he flew. One called to another and said:
> "Holy, holy, holy is the Lord of hosts;
> the whole earth is full of his glory." (Isaiah 6:1-3, RSV).

This passage from the sixth chapter of Isaiah is certainly one of the

125

best-known in a book filled, as we have said, with familiar prophecies. And, because it is so well-known, it often suffers from weak reading. But, just look at all of the images we, as liturgists, have to deal with in those brief lines! The Lord on his throne, the entire company of those who form his court, the seraphim. Of course, before we can begin, we have to know what a seraph is. A trip to the dictionary tells us:

> seraph: one of the 6-winged angels of the highest rank believed in ancient Judaism to guard God's throne with sacred ardor.[2]

Then we need to *visualize* such a divine being: see the six wings, watch the angelic flight, hear, and *re-create for our listeners* the *sound* of the angel voices. We must dare—we must be willing to enter into the drama of the scene as fully as Isaiah himself did. Only then can we move our listeners to the emotion of the moment. This use of richly colorful language is not unique to Isaiah and Ezekiel. The re-creation of such visions becomes our task throughout all the books of prophecy.

The prophetic writings themselves have been referred to as an anthology of anthologies. As we have said, they are a gathering of notes and remembrances—reminders of the righteousness of Yahweh and his power. And because these works are collections we often have trouble finding any sort of unity between these writings, and even within some of the books themselves. Certainly there is none of the cohesiveness we found in the structured arguments of the epistles. The only unifying factor seems to be the intensity of vision we get from the prophets themselves.

An Example from Amos

While time, place, and historical circumstances are impossible to detail with any certainty, we must keep some sense of the *approximate* time and the situation which gave rise to these pronouncements. We need an awareness of the wars, the desolations, the social problems that beset the children of Israel, and their hope for Yahweh's intervention in their behalf. For example, Amos' words were spoken in a time of great wealth and luxury for Israel. The rich lived for their own pleasure. They were corrupt, decadent, and vicious in their dealings with those around them. Amos spoke out against their self-indulgence and called for social justice and a return to older, simpler ways. The echoes of Amos' words still ring in our own ears today.

His style is vivid. Early in the book, he begins no less than eight stanzas with the names of different cities, localities and tribes whom the Lord has condemned: "Thus says the LORD: 'For three transgressions of Damascus (Gaza, the Ammorites) and for four, I will not revoke the punishment. . . .'" And, even though we may not be conversant with the crimes of the peoples and places named, as were those who formed Amos' audiences, we need to react to the punishment which awaits them. In subsequent sections he begins nearly every stanza or unit with, "These are the words of the Lord" or "This is what the Lord showed me." At times Amos sounds almost like Paul in his use of rhetorical questions. Listen to this passage from chapter 3:

Hear this word that the Lord has spoken against you,
O people of Israel, against the whole family which I brought up out
of the land of Egypt:
   "You only have I known
   of all the families of the earth;
   therefore I will punish you
   for all your iniquities.
Do two walk together, unless they have made an appointment?
Does a lion roar in the forest when he has no prey?
Does a young lion cry out from his den, if he has taken nothing?
Does a bird fall in a snare on the earth, when there is no trap for it?
Is a trumpet blown in a city, and the people are not afraid?
Does evil befall a city, unless the Lord has done it?
Surely the Lord GOD does nothing without revealing his secret to
   his servants the prophets.
The lion has roared; who will not fear?
The Lord GOD has spoken; who can but prophesy?"
(Amos 3:1–8, RSV)

The repeated questions, of course, produce identical and irrefutable answers. So, when Amos reaches the final question, "who can but prophesy?" there is no choice here either.

Poetic Quality—Micah

In addition to the rhetorical style of the prophecies, we also need to respond to the *poetry* of these passages. We spoke in the last chapter of the need in the epistles to mark stressed and unstressed syllables to determine the speech rhythms of some passages. It is even more important to hear the melodies of speech in the prophecies. The music/poetry of these sections is as significant to our effective sharing with our listeners as is intelligent awareness of the content.

In most contemporary translations the book of Micah is transcribed entirely in the form of poetry—arranged in lyric form on the page. And, while the usual marks of English poetry, such as rhyme scheme and meter, are missing, as they must be in a translation like this, the language still reads with the sensory appeal and the vitality of a good poem. We can look at chapter 6 as one example of Micah's poetic style. The pattern of arrangement on the page is what we would expect from a poem. But to deal with the *content* in this chapter we need to know that, unlike many of the other prophets, Micah was not accustomed to city life; he really did not trust it. In this book, he turns his lyric technique to express his attitude as he rails at both the sins of cities and the duplicity he found there. In this sixth chapter we find Micah at his best as he provides his listeners with the great contrasts he finds between God's natural world and life in the city. The word choices contrast the two worlds in ways that challenge our responses to the content and to our own versatility as lectors in our abilities to respond to the way in which this content is expressed. Micah begins the chapter by saying:

Hear what the Lord says:
Arise, plead your case before the mountains,
and let the hills hear your voice (Micah 6:1, RSV)

He follows with the question that confronts all of us:

With what shall I come before the Lord,
and bow myself before God on high?
Shall I come before him with burnt offerings,
with calves a year old? (Micah 6:6, RSV)

He begins an exercise in exaggeration as he speaks of "thousands of rams" and "ten thousand rivers of oil." He asks: "Shall I give my first-born for my transgression . . . for the sin of my soul?" Then he concludes this section/stanza with lovely poetry of the sort we have heard so often in other parts of the book:

> He has showed you, O man, what is good;
> and what does the Lord require of you
> but to do justice, and love kindness,
> and to walk humbly with your God (Micah 6:8).

Then, in one of those difficult transitions (perhaps it is a later editor's comment), he begins to point out the problems inherent in the cities. "The voice of the Lord cries to the cities. . . ." He goes on to list what are certainly his own problems with city life—scales that give short measure, people who lie for their own benefit, rich men who are "full of violence."

We need to take the time to listen, and respond, to the wonderful images Micah builds in this book. We need to work out the changes in rhythm as that rhythm reinforces the content established by the words. This book really yields its richest rewards for us and for our listeners when we give in to the poetry and let it sing.

We previously commented on Isaiah and his very graphic picture of his call to serve as a prophet for the Lord. Like both Amos and Micah, Isaiah was a prominent man in his country's affairs. He was a counselor to kings for over thirty years, we are told. But when he turns to prophecy, his words proclaim the destruction of Israel and of Judah and the punishment of the nation for its infidelity. For ten chapters, Isaiah proclaims "oracles" portending the destruction or punishments of the nations surrounding Israel—from Assyria to Egypt. His words ring clear for thirty-nine chapters. But, at chapter forty, the language and the content changes. This change in tone and content accounts for one of the reasons scholars usually refer to a "second Isaiah" speaking in the last portion of the book.

The "Second Isaiah"

This section of the prophecy is usually assigned to the period of Israel's exile. Scholars base their judgments on two areas of content in

129

this latter part. First are the passages which have been titled the "Suffering Servant" or "Servant of Yahweh" sections (42:1–4; 49:5–10; 52:13–15 and 53:12 in the RSV translation). In these sections, the prophet tells us that God has chosen a Servant, unnamed, but apparently a person from the nation, who will bear the burden of redeeming the whole people.

Further, almost every page in the last twenty-seven chapters contains familiar words of consolation, assurance, and promise of redemption. So reassuring is it that this section is often called the "Book of Consolation." From the opening words of chapter forty: "Comfort, comfort my people, says your God," to the twenty-second verse of chapter sixty-six, which speaks of the "new heaven and new earth," we hear the prophet assuring the exiles. God has not deserted his people. A better day lies ahead. One of the major problems in these last chapters is the one we have mentioned so often before—the problem of *familiarity*. We no longer dare to just give *breath* to these words, rather, we must bring them to *life*, filling them with the threats, the consolation, and the promise which fills them.

"Inspired" Writers

We have spoken of the need to do some work on the sensory images and the poetic style of these books of prophecy, and, technically, this work is important. But there is one major imperative that looms above all the rest. It is that we read all of these prophecies with the rich certainty of an inspired individual.

It is very difficult to resist the temptation to look at each of the books of prophecy in terms of content and organization, because each presents his own unique way of speaking God's word to the people of the prophet's time and place. You will find similarities among some of them, as well as differences.

Technically speaking, Moses was probably the greatest of the prophets in the history of Israel. His commands came from God in face-to-face—or, more accurately, "face-to-back" interviews, as God gave Moses the laws, instructed him in the ritual of worship even to the arrangement of candles in standards. He was directed on the journey through forty years in the wilderness and in many other matters, both spiritual and practical. A major difference between the accounts of Moses' encounters with God, his pronouncements, and those of the later prophets is that, in Moses' prophecies, they are all reported by the third-person narrator, not by the man himself. But, then, he was "slow of speech," we are told. The first transition to the "first-person" style of the later prophets comes with the book of Daniel. Here, most of the events are reported in third person, but the visions themselves are delivered in Daniel's own voice.

One of the persistent traps for us, as liturgists, lies in the rapid transitions from one idea or image to the next. Often there is no resolution to the story or description of a city's or nation's behavior. The story line often turns from the event to the prophet's own actions. The lesson is always for the present although the events themselves took place in the past, or sometimes the future. They are often so highly dramatic as to be part of another world entirely.

The prophets' compulsion to speak gives the writings an intensity we must not ignore. They did not waste time with long introductions. They take immediate command and tell us directly whose attention God demands. They speak from immediate experience. The happenings and conversations are reported directly, increasing the immediacy of the experience. Yahweh speaks in his own person through the prophet, and the words are his. The prophets were convinced that they had been called to serve as mouthpieces of the Lord. They did not speak for themselves; God spoke through them. They were able to see the future as well as the past and present through God's eyes. They were a unique phenomenon and although today's listeners may have difficulty accepting their words as factual, they were nevertheless an important part of history and first-rate speakers. The clues to their effectiveness lie in the links they make between the world of people and the world God envisions for people. Congregations must *not* be made to suffer through scholarly commentary and "footnotes" during the process of hearing the words of the Lord, as proclaimed by his prophets. The prophecies stand as they are. They demand only that we communicate them fully.

Visions and Sensory Images

For many worship leaders the *visions* we find in the prophecies are a problem. How can we possibly make a modern congregation believe them? This is a case of selling those old story-tellers short. The visions have so much action—so many sights and sounds—that all we have to do is *respond* to all that imagery in order for the visions to become real and present. This is the opportunity we are given in this age where the human imagination is left out of the entertainment packages presented on the electronic media. When we let our voices respond to the words—shaping and creating the sights and sounds—when we let our bodies respond to the feelings of action, both external and "under the skin," then our listeners will be caught up in the adventure of the visions. *But we must allow ourselves to become involved, creating the images within ourselves first.*

Every type of sensory imagery is to be found both in the visions and on every page of the prophecies. The style is solemn, often even obscure to modern ears. It, in fact, matches the pronouncements of the oracles we find in most of these books. But we find our senses being bombarded by the descriptive words we find. This brief passage from Isaiah 40:3 (NRSV) shows just a bit of this:

> A voice cries out:
> "In the wilderness prepare the way of the LORD,
> make straight in the desert a highway for our God.
> Every valley shall be lifted up,
> and every mountain and hill be made low;
> the uneven ground shall become level,
> and the rough places a plain.
> Then the glory of the LORD shall be revealed,
> and all people shall see it together,
> for the mouth of the LORD has spoken it."

The visual images alone will keep our listeners' attention. Just look at them! The words "wilderness," "desert," "highway," "valley," "mountain," uneven ground," "rough places," and "plain" need only our own visualization of them in order for the congregation to see them through our eyes. The *sounds* of the "voice" that cries out begins the passage, and the fact that "the mouth of the LORD has spoken it" ends it. In between are "action/sensation" words like the image of valleys being *lifted up* and mountains and hills being "made low." The whole passage rolls to a sensory climax as the prophet uses *kinesthetic*, "under the skin" action with the feelings we get from the word "glory"; we see the glory "revealed" and "all people shall see it." As we just noted, the images are given the final seal of authority as "the mouth of the LORD has spoken."

We need not be afraid to respond to these images as fully as we can. We will not become too dramatic so long as we *remain absolutely true to the text itself*. Only when we interject our own comment, by projecting our own acting abilities, appliquéing technique on top of text, will the effectiveness of the passage be destroyed. Some of the lections, especially those using third-person narrators, contain "stage directions" to tell us that someone shouted, or spoke in a loud voice. We must use these cues just as an actor does. This is the way it sounded; we have to make it sound that way now.

The prophets of the Hebrew scriptures were not terrified when they heard the Lord speaking to them. They undoubtedly were struck with awe that they had been chosen, but they did not run and hide. They had been chosen. God spoke through them and they speak today through whoever reads them aloud. Both the speaker and his point of view are clearly defined, and both of these awarenesses are basic to effective reading of these texts.

The Book of Revelation

Has there ever been a book more misused than this one? Passages have been cited to prove the place of Satan in societies from Rome to the former Soviet Union. Even items of daily use have been targeted as evil signs in our world.[3] The signs and symbols do offer tempting material for misreaders to select as indicators of the presence of evil in our world. It is not surprising then, that, given the complexities of language—the sights and sounds with which the book is filled—Martin Luther should have written in his preface to the German translation in 1522:

> They are supposed to be blessed who keep what is written in this book; and yet, no one knows what that is, to say nothing of keeping it. This is just the same as if we did not have the book at all. And there are many far better books available for us to keep.[4]

As we read Revelation today, we may agree with Luther. It is certainly true that, for us as lectors, the demands which the language makes on

133

us often seem overwhelming. The text is no less formidable. But, as Charles Giblin, S.J., writes: "The interpreter's task is to read the text aright and, at the same time, to enable his audience to assimilate and savor the text which John has laid out before us."[5] To do so will require close attention and, usually, some outside reading in one or more of the many commentaries on the book.

The attributions of prophecy for modern times have shrouded and encumbered the book for centuries. Those ascriptions aside, we, as liturgists, must first and foremost be attentive to the structure and the demands the language makes on us as we read it aloud. There is no denying that this is exciting and dramatic reading. But we must keep to the intent that most scholars see as basic to the writing. The Revelation which John envisions in this book is the epitome of apocalyptic literature. It is a statement of hope, a song of future victory based on God's promise of peace for his people. That pledge is rooted in the Hebrew scriptures. It begins in the book of Exodus and is repeated in the Christian scripture by Jesus, whose last words reported in Matthew's gospel are: "And know that I am with you always, until the end of the world!" (Matt 28:20, NAB). John's vision restates the assurance that God will keep his people safe, creating a new world of hope and of joy.

Most scholars agree that Revelation is a continuation of similar apocalyptic writing which began to appear around 200 BC. As William Barclay writes:

> It is not an isolated book, although there is nothing like it in the New Testament. It belongs to a class of literature which was common between the Testaments. All these books are wild and unintelligible, for they are all visions of a time in which no man knew what would happen, and they are all trying to describe the indescribable and to put into words that which is beyond words. . . . and our book is one of them; and the very subject with which it deals is the reason it is so difficult to understand.[6]

While the writing is unique in the Bible, Revelation does share a characteristic we have encountered before. The authorship of this volume has been a subject for discussion among scholars for a very long time. Is the John whose name appears in the first lines of the book also the John of the gospel and whose name is associated with the epistles of

John? As early as A.D. 250, Dionysius, Bishop of Alexandria, refused to accept that notion. For one thing, the generally accepted date(s) for the book range between A.D. 90 and 95, which would have made the apostle John a very old man indeed. Further, as Barclay points out, the John of this text refers to himself as a prophet. If he had been one of the Twelve, Barclay suggests, he would undoubtedly have used his apostolic title instead. So, for most scholars, the author remains "John of Patmos."

As we noted earlier, like the prophecies, Revelation proclaims the final triumph of God and the establishment of a new and perfect order for his people. One notable difference between this book and the earlier disclosures is that the prophecies were proclaimed orally; Revelation began, and has continued to be, a *written* work. The differences are not nearly so great for us as they are for the scholars. The language of this text flows with as much vitality and energy as we will find anywhere in the Bible. Ezekiel, with his vivid use of form and color, and Zechariah with his visions of animals and strange beasts come immediately to mind as we read this book. But the book is uneven in its construction. There are breaks in the sequence of ideas and in their development, breaks which may puzzle and vex us as we prepare our readings. These discrepancies have led scholars to some interesting conclusions.[7]

For our purpose the book works well when we have some understanding of the content and when we read it aloud. In a vision there is no real need to follow a realistic or orderly sequence of events. There is only the need to follow the twisting, sometimes broken, thread of the narrative. Our task is the re-creation of the text as fully as we can.

As we approach reading from Revelation we seem to find ourselves, momentarily at least, back with the structure of the letters which formed the preaching/teaching style basic to Paul's work. The book begins with a kind of preface to the letters themselves in which John describes his call to prophesy. There follows a series of seven epistles to "the seven churches that are in Asia," the major churches that existed in the Roman province of that name.[8] Although the "seven churches that are in Asia" did exist, we need to be aware that we are not reading historical documents. Rather, like the prophecies of Hebrew scripture, these are brief, instructive pamphlets which were written under specific circumstances for particular audiences. The infant church was struggling, facing persecution from the secular community and disturbances within the churches themselves. So the book is really a prediction of the triumph of God and his continued assurances of that outcome.

The letters themselves have a pattern to them. Each begins with an identical salutation/warning from "one like a son of man." We need to be aware that this formula opening needs vocal and intellectual variety if we are reading more than one of these letters at a single service. And each epistle ends with the words, "He who has an ear, let him hear what the Spirit says to the churches," followed by an assurance of reward which will be given, "To him who conquers." These last sentences also have a pattern, a style to them, since they are the final unifying factor for all seven letters.

The writing which follows the letters is rich to overflowing in symbolism, but the material must not be taken on a literal level. Fire, blood and darkness are contrasted to the white of angelic robes and the brilliance of heavenly light. The symbols often make it difficult for us to comprehend what John has in mind, but he is careful to explain some of the things which often seem obscure in the text. There is the mysticism of the often-repeated number seven and the meaning of some of the animals in his vision. The writer is reporting an awesome and exhilarating event, so explanations are necessary to make the experience as clear to his readers as he can. We find ourselves in a forgotten landscape dotted with semi-precious stones. The colors are unfamiliar to most of us, but we find they fit the mood of the places John describes.

As the story moves into the second major part, what Giblin refers to as "John's Heavenly, Universal Vision of Things to Come Hereafter," we find that we are provided with clear transitional indications. Phrases like, "After this I looked," and "Next I saw," help us—and our listeners—to be aware of the shifts in time and place that are taking place. We need to see these words and phrases for what they are, transitions from one place or time to another. They help our congregations follow the narrative as we step into the next vision.

The second major section is further divided into units of seven—seven unsealings of the scroll, trumpet blasts, and libation bowls. And within each we are challenged to reconstruct the sights and the sounds contained in each unit. John assists us by providing "stage directions" in many places. We are told to read parts of the narrative of the "Heavenly Worship" section as it is sung—"without ceasing," "with full voice." Do we dare? Each lector and each congregation will determine the degree to which these directions will be followed. Other notes on performance are easier; 6:1 says the four living creatures "call out, as with a voice of thunder;" 6:10 says the souls of the slaughtered "cried out with a loud voice." Even if we choose not to follow the "directions," these cues can be of value to us in getting the spirit and feeling of the passages we are bringing to life.

6:12 brings with it a major switch in focus. For eleven verses we have focused on images of sound. Now the pattern shifts. All the images are of sight. John speaks of garments "black as sackcloth," things that "become like blood." Visual/action images appear: "as a fig tree drops winter fruit." These pictures continue until the opening of the seventh seal. The sounds of trumpets and voices stand in marked contrast to the "silence in Heaven" which follows the opening of the seventh seal. But the shift is brief. John recommences the strong physical image patterns, first with sight, "golden trumpets" and "golden censers," followed by the smell and sight of clouds of incense. Then comes fire, "peals of thunder, rumblings, flashes of lightning, and an earthquake" (8:5). From this point on until the Epilogue and Benediction, the text demands close attention and response to all of the sensory appeals ever used in literature.

There is an interesting shift in point of view at the beginning of chapter 10. John is visited by an angel. He is cautioned against revealing certain things, while being told that he can reveal others. Then he is given a measuring rod and becomes an active participant in the events that follow. He returns to his role of spectator and auditor for the next two visions. He is drawn into the proceedings again in chapter 17, where he remains through 18:11.

On first reading, the book of Revelation seems to be overflowing with all types of imagery. In fact, it is primarily visual and auditory. Things are reported as seen and heard.

It is from the physical responses we make to these visions and sounds that we will draw the inspirations to bring the whole panorama to life for our listeners. From all of this it is apparent that Revelation can make both exciting and moving reading for us and for our congregations. It seems somewhat neglected in these days. Perhaps in our century we are afraid of emotions, and we do not respond easily to wonder and delight. Perhaps Revelation is too often considered a series of horrors. Taken as a whole, however, it is a dramatic restatement of the belief that has endured since Exodus that God would be with "his people."

Revelation is based on the principle of contrasts. The thunder and fire must be kept in balance with the setting of the seal, the hymns of praise, and the bright lights of glory. It is a spectacular vision in larger-than-living color told by one who saw and heard it first-hand. It may make the modern theologians cringe at the naivete of this picture, but it makes for good reading and good listening. Like the prophecies of Hebrew scripture, it needs to be read as a document written by a person who was under divine directive to share his experiences with his people.

Notes

1. *Webster's Seventh New Collegiate Dictionary* (Springfield, Mass.: G. & C. Merriam Co., 1971),p. 41. Italics and materials in brackets added.

2. *Webster's Seventh New Collegiate Dictionary*, p. 741

3. Richard Jeske, in his book *Revelation for Today: Images of Hope* (Philadelphia: Fortress Press, 1983, p. 3), cites an unusual, if not unexpected, one. " . . . a little tract has circulated recently which contends that the Universal Product Code marks on grocery items used in rapid-price scanning systems are foretold in Rev. 13:17: ' . . . no one can buy or sell unless he has the mark, that is, the name of the beast or the number of its name.' In other words, such marking systems are, according to the anonymous author of this tract, another example of the growing and pervasive influence of the "beast," namely Satan, in the world today."

4. cited in Jeske, p. 10.

5. Charles H. Giblin, S.J., *The Book of Revelation: The Open Book of Prophecy* (Collegeville, MN: The Liturgical Press, 1991), p.8.

6 William Barclay, *The Revelation of John: Volume 1* (Philadelphia: The Westminster Press, 1959), p. 27.

7. One of these is that there were two separate apocalypses written by the same author but at different times. The two, they say, were later fused into one book.

8. The area consisted of the eastern end of the Mediterranean coast in the area now known as Turkey.

10

Reviewing the Process
of Preparing

In the preceding chapters we have endeavored to provide you with the theories and the rationale for understanding *why* you do what you do when you serve as a worship leader, liturgist or lector. What follows here is a guide to preparation—a summary of *how* you prepare to read the scriptures aloud for an audience.

Taking the Assignment

Having agreed (perhaps in a weak moment) to serve as a lector/ liturgist/worship leader you may have awakened to some fears about where to begin.

Step One: Choose the translation you prefer, a translation that is intellectually accessible to you and to your audience. Ask your pastor if there is a preferred translation for this service. You undoubtedly have a favorite copy, a copy you have read for some time. With your pastor's help, agree on the version you will use.

Start by reading the assigned passage there. Then, perhaps, you will want to read another translation—maybe even two more—just to look at any differences which may occur. Choose the one that speaks best to you and fits with the sermon topic of the morning.

Step Two: Read it all.

The probabilities are that your selections are only parts of larger, longer chapters. So. . .

1. Read the entire chapter. By doing so you will learn how your assigned readings fit into the context of the whole discourse.

2. Note the location of the reading. Does it begin the chapter? If so, what material forms the balance of the chapter? If the reading is in the middle, what precedes and what follows it? Is your selection the "heart" of the story? Obviously, if you are reading the last section, you need to be aware of all that has led up to this point in the chapter and, perhaps, even in the book.

Step Three: Consult.

Consult your pastor. Find out how this passage is being used in the development of the morning's homily or sermon.

You may find that, even after talking with the pastor, you still want more information or more scholarship about the reading. Your church library is a good place to start. You might begin by looking at some of the commentaries on the passage. There are many good books to help you learn more about the reading, the chapter, the entire book. Many of the commentaries have brief descriptive statements about various passages. The material you find here will help to broaden your understanding of the reading and will provide you with material you may want to use in your introduction.

There may be allusions about which you are unsure. Check a concordance. You will learn from it how the Old and New Testaments interlock. Some New Testament sections are seen as validations of Old Testament prophecy. You may then wish to read both testaments to see how the connections work.

Step Four: Prepare your reading.

Read through the text two or three times to be sure you understand it, then:

(a). Make a double-spaced copy of the passage (or passages) you are reading. The first purpose is to familiarize yourself with the text. Copying the words seems to set them in order in your mind. The double-spaced copy makes an ideal rehearsal script. You can underline important words; you can make marginal notes. You can divide sentences into speech phrases, which, in turn, helps you read the sense of the selection. The typescript becomes your "workbench" in preparation for you performance.

(b). Check pronunciations. As we said in an earlier chapter, if you are unsure about the pronunciation of any word, check with a dictionary and then with your pastor. If the name or word appears in the

140

text of the sermon, you both will be happiest if you agree on the way it is said.

You may also choose to use the copy for your reading(s) during the service itself. It is difficult for most of us to read from an average-sized Bible, especially when the reading is done under the pressure of a service in a public setting.

Step Five: Prepare the introduction.

1. Your audience needs to know more than just the chapter, verse, and translation you are using. An introduction prepares your audience to listen carefully. The introduction gives them background on the selection, the events that have preceded, the people involved. They will better remember the reading when it becomes the base for the sermon/homily which follows, so. . .

2. In consultation with your pastor, point the audience toward the sermon topic. Understand that you are not providing the message of the morning; you are John the Baptist, preparing the way for the "word of the Lord."

3. Write out your introduction. Rehearse it three or four times, until you are comfortable with it.

Throw it away!

You must let the introduction seem spontaneous—as it should be. The inspiration of the words of the scripture will be working on you right up until you begin. Be willing to let new insights come to you, even while you are speaking.

Step Six: Rehearse.

1. Read the passage aloud and alone. Read it enough times that you are sure of every element in it. Do not be in doubt about either the pronunciation or the meaning of a single word! Check a dictionary if you are unsure of any word's meaning. An audience knows immediately when you do not understand what you are saying. And when that happens, the audience mentally checks out and leaves you reading to yourself.

2. Read the passage(s) aloud for a trusted friend. You need some feedback from someone who will be helpful. If you wish, and if you can arrange the time, read for your pastor. The important thing is that you get some sort of response before you read for an audience.

3. Unless you are accustomed to reading for large groups, or have served as liturgist/lector before, read your selection(s) in the church

and from the lectern you will be using. It is very important that you get used to the sound of the room. Rehearsal in the sanctuary (or wherever you will be reading) will help you discover how much volume you need to reach that hard-of-hearing person who always seems to sit near the back of the room. You will find that you have to adjust your speech rate. We spoke in chapter 2 about voice projection. Reread the section, then use the ideas in there to help you reach the back row, but to do it without shouting.

Check out the sound system, if any. How will you best be able to use the microphone? How close or far from you must it be? Get used to the sound of your voice as it is amplified. It will NOT sound like what you are used to. Don't be surprised by the difference only when you begin to read in the service.

4. Get comfortable in the space you will be using.

Step Seven: Relax!

You and your pastor are in agreement about how the reading fits into the experience of worship. You have reviewed the scholarship. You have prepared your introduction. You know how to use the space in which you will be reading. Now, direct your energies into the words you are sharing as part of the worship experience of the day.

Let the Light shine!

SO WHAT!!

A Sort of Epilogue

Regularly in our teaching, the words "So What?" have appeared at the end of written class assignments. And just as regularly students ask, "What does that mean?" The best answer has been: "What have you learned from this assignment?"

In the preface you read our belief that no one should be bored hearing these books read aloud. Now, at the conclusion of our sharing with you, here are some answers to the "So What?" question, answers you may have found as you prepare to share the scriptures with the people of your church.

First and foremost, you may have found that the Bible is human. It was written by humans for humans. As such, it is meant to be shared as completely, as emotionally and as intellectually as possible. It is this sharing that vitalizes well-worn passages, giving them life again.

You may have discovered some of the myriad ways the excitement, the humor, the inspiration of these pages can be brought to life for people today.

You probably have found that reading both the scriptures and the commentaries on them has deepened your understanding, as well as your delight and your commitment to share the writings.

We would like to believe you have found new satisfaction in reading the Bible for your own pleasure.

From the experience of many other liturgists with whom we have shared these ideas, it seems clear that personal reading develops more personal understanding. Armed with that knowledge, sharing the words with others, then listening/watching their responses, our joy as lectors is increased manyfold. After we have done a good job with a much-used passage from the Bible, and someone says after a service, "I never heard those words—really heard them—before," we receive one of those intangible "fringe benefits" skilled liturgists can experience.

Perhaps your work with the language of the Bible has made you aware of new physical and emotional responses which are available to you as you read all literary forms. You may have discovered reactions and feelings you had never considered before when you have read scripture. Your body may have found new freedom to express the inner feelings that are part of every good lection.

Have you found that the vocal exercises give you more confidence in the quality and range of your voice?

Good!

These are all "pluses" which will add to your general reading pleasure.

But our most important wish is for you to feel you have become a better messenger of the "good news." In the vernacular, "That's what it's all about."

All teachers like to believe that students who have studied with them will become standard-bearers of the ideas and knowledge the teachers have put before them. We are no different. It is our sincere hope that you will illuminate the Bible for your parishes and your congregations, that you will bring new insight and inspiration to your listeners, that you will share your new-found expertise with those who share the lectern with you.

So you have come to the end of this book, but you are just beginning your adventure in service and in faith.

There are many "final words" that could be shared with you, many blessings you have heard in services for years, such as, "The Lord bless you and keep you . . ." and others distinct to your own church experience. But our benediction is one which is sung during the Sabbath service in Fiddler on the Roof:

> May the Lord protect and defend you
> May the Lord preserve you from pain.
> Favor them, O Lord,
> With happiness and peace.
> O hear our Sabbath prayer.
> Amen.